DE

***A**s for me and my household, we will serve the Lord.*

—Joshua 24:15

SEPTEMBER

Photo © Comstock

Gary Allen, Editor

Everything in Order

As long as the earth endures, seedtime and harvest, cold and heat, summer and winter, day and night will never cease (Genesis 8:22).

Scripture: **Genesis 8:13-22**
Song: **"He Has Never Failed Me Yet"**

What if you looked out at the nighttime sky and saw about 20 comets and meteors hurtling through the velvety darkness, headed your way? Of course, once in a great while a meteor does thud onto our planet. However, by and large, we don't face such chaotic randomness. Our universe runs pretty fixedly.

God has signified that fixity as we see it in the four seasons. True, during my five years of living in southern California, we may have had about one rain for perhaps three days straight. But even there we still had the regular rhythm of predictable seasons. So Genesis 8:22 is a handle to hold onto; we have a God of order.

An excellent application for us comes through in 1 Corinthians 14:40, which advocates doing everything in an orderly way. Do I show up on time for my appointments? Can people bank on my word? These are some of the questions I ask myself as I ponder God's trustworthiness in my life and in His running of the entire universe.

Lord, *enable me to mirror Your orderly faithfulness. Through Christ, my Lord and Savior, I pray. Amen.*

September 1–3. **Jim Townsend** of Elgin, Illinois, spends his time teaching college classes, preaching on Sundays, and writing all manner of Christian literature.

Enjoy It All!

Everything that lives and moves will be food for you. Just as I gave you the green plants, I now give you everything (Genesis 9:3).

Scripture: **Genesis 9:1-7**
Song: **"Break Thou the Bread of Life"**

Funny what we remember. I can still recall a particular hamburger I ate years ago in a little out-of-the-way restaurant in San Diego's Old Town. And in a German restaurant in San Francisco, I consumed the most wonderful sauerbraten. And there was the sliced roast beef cooked outdoors in Memphis, Tennessee, at a church picnic (remembered from my childhood). No wonder I relish the words of 1 Timothy 6:17—that God has lavishly supplied us with "everything for our enjoyment." G. K. Chesterton said that he even "enjoyed his enjoyment."

In Genesis 9:3 God permitted humanity to enjoy a vegetable-plus diet. Of course, the medical profession may need to warn us that a heavy diet of bacon, sausage, and other red meat is not so hot for our hearts. Still, I'm glad that Genesis 9:3 is in the Bible. It tells me that God has made our palates for the pleasurable.

We also need to remember the palates of the needy. Meanwhile, thank God for roast beef and charbroiled lamb chops (don't forget to add the mint jelly).

Thank You, Lord, *that so many of us don't have to go hungry. You've even given us variety. And help us to remember the Golden Rule when it comes to food. In the name of Christ I pray. Amen.*

September 3

No Arrow Here

I have set my rainbow in the clouds, and it will be the sign of the covenant between me and the earth (Genesis 9:13).

Scripture: **Genesis 9:8-17**
Song: **"There's a Light upon the Mountains"**

Lucy and I were sitting on Lake Avenue (on restaurant row) in Pasadena, California, when we happened to have one of our rare California rains. Since the sun was shining brightly, you know what we could see in the sky.

Believe it or not, if I had had a camera then, I could have raked in big bucks with a unique shot. Why? The rainbow we saw in the sky ended not in a pot of gold, but in the bucket of that famous fast-food chicken place right across the street!

God is pro-rainbows. But have you noticed that a rainbow *is* a bow—but without any arrow in it? God has set this weapon of warfare up in the sky, but He has signaled us that all that might be menacing is missing. There is no arrow of anger aimed at us.

God has made His armistice and peace treaty at Christ's cross. The cross is almost a plus sign; it's positive. God is *for us* (Romans 8:31).

A little rainbow never hurt anybody. As God washed Noah's world clean, so He can wash our hearts clean with His forgiving love.

Bless You, Lord, *for Your full and free forgiveness. Help me to laugh in belief the next time I spot a rainbow. I pray this prayer in the name of Jesus, my merciful Savior and Lord. Amen.*

Sources of Encouragement

We who have fled to take hold of the hope offered to us may be greatly encouraged (Hebrews 6:18).

Scripture: **Hebrews 6:13-20**
Song: **"Trusting Jesus"**

David Brainerd, an eighteenth-century missionary to the American Indians, died of tuberculosis at age 29. Jonathan Edwards later published Brainerd's diary, which spoke of spiritual struggles, weakness from his disease, frequent fastings, and his burden for lost souls. Missionary William Carey took a copy of the book with him to India. Though Brainerd was no longer alive, his steadfast faith in the midst of trials served to encourage Carey.

In an effort to encourage Jewish Christians, the writer of the book of Hebrews used the example of Abraham's faith. Though Abraham and Sarah had no children, God told Abraham he would have many descendants. For 25 years Abraham waited for his first child.

Had God forgotten? No, Abraham could hold tight to God's promise. In the same way, the discouraged Hebrews could count on God's unchanging nature; He cannot lie. When we struggle to believe, observing the lives of other faithful believers can make all the difference.

Dear God, *I thank You for the testimonies of believers who kept the faith amid severe circumstances. In Jesus' name, amen.*

September 4–10. **Jewell Johnson** writes from Arizona where she enjoys walking, reading, and quilting. She and her husband, LeRoy, have seven grandchildren.

Pilgrim Attitude

They were longing for a better country—a heavenly one (Hebrews 11:16).

Scripture: **Hebrews 11:8-16**
Song: **"What a Day That Will Be"**

"There it is! I see the big wheel!" I yelled from the back seat of the car when I saw the Ferris wheel in the distance. The county fair was the biggest event of the summer for my brothers and me when we were kids. We talked about it for months, saved our money for the concessions, and wore new outfits for the occasion.

Anticipation comprises much of the pleasure of any enjoyable event. At the beginning of his journey, Abraham didn't fully comprehend his destination. He lived in tents among strange peoples, often his enemies. He believed God for a son even when Sarah was old and barren. He obeyed God even when the instructions he received did not seem to make sense, because he looked beyond his situation to Heaven, to a better place.

No one is sick in Heaven. No one dies. There are no prisons or crime. Rather, that better country has mansions, rivers, fruit trees, the saints of all ages, and Jesus our Savior. Think about it, read about it, dream about that place as Abraham did. What will it be like to live forever with your Lord?

Heavenly Father, *as a pilgrim on this earth, I shade my eyes and look toward Heaven's horizon. Thank You for this hope of a better world to come. Let its vision strengthen my courage today. In the name of Jesus, amen.*

The Heavens Speak

Look up at the heavens and count the stars—if indeed you can count them (Genesis 15:5).

Scripture: **Genesis 15:1-6**
Song: **"Look, Ye Saints! The Sight Is Glorious"**

As a child I lived in an area where, on cold winter nights, the flickering, shifting northern lights put on a display comparable to fireworks. In summer, the Milky Way galaxy, with its billions of stars, caused me to ooh and aah.

God often gets our attention through nature. When He wanted to assure Abram that He would make of him a great nation, He took him outside on a clear night for a lesson from the heavens. Although Abram and Sarai had no children, God told Abram that his descendants would someday be as numerous as the stars. Abram reasoned that his heir would be his trusted servant Eliezer. No, God said. The heir would come from Abram's own body.

I wonder what it was like to hear God's voice while gazing at the myriad shining lights overhead. In the future, when I can't figure out how God will fulfill my heart's deepest desire, I'm going to try counting stars. I can remember that my awesome creator merely spoke, and galaxies appeared. Surely He will give good things to all who place their trust in Him.

Lord, *assure me today that I am constantly in Your mind. Your love for me is greater than the galaxies, and Your blessings as numberless as the stars. I place my whole life in Your hands! In Jesus' name, amen.*

Inner-Circle Friendship

You, however, will go to your fathers in peace and be buried at a good old age (Genesis 15:15).

Scripture: **Genesis 15:12-21**
Song: **"What a Friend We Have in Jesus"**

Joanne and I became acquainted through work, but we didn't have an in-depth conversation until the day she shared with me about her family's problems: a daughter suffering an abusive marriage, a son threatening suicide. In turn, I told Joanne about our daughter's struggle with an eating disorder. As we wept together and comforted one another, we became good friends, bonded by common difficulties.

Abram (Abraham) was called the friend of God (2 Chronicles 20:7). He asked God questions, and God told him of things to come. His descendants, God said, would be in slavery for 400 years, but the nation that enslaved them would be punished. As a true friend, God comforted Abram, assuring him that he wouldn't live to see the impending sorrow. And after four generations, his nation would return to their land.

Often deep friendships develop from shared problems. While it may be difficult to find someone we can trust with our deepest cares, Jesus is such a person. As we regularly share our concerns with Him, He becomes our most trusted inner circle friend.

Dear Lord, *thank You for listening intently to my cares and concerns today. You are my Savior and friend. I love You! In Christ I pray. Amen.*

He Sees

She gave this name to the LORD who spoke to her: "You are the God who sees me," for she said, "I have now seen the One who sees me" (Genesis 16:13).

Scripture: **Genesis 16:1-15**
Song: **"'Tis So Sweet to Trust in Jesus"**

Fifteen-year-old Lori, distraught because her mother had remarried, left home and headed for Mexico. In a small town on the border, she became afraid and called a minister who eventually reunited Lori with her mother, thus sparing the family further suffering.

Family conflicts also caused Hagar to flee from home. Her mistress, Sarai, frustrated because she had no children, suggested to Abram that he have a child by the slave girl. He agreed. But when Hagar became pregnant, she began to despise her mistress. In turn, Sarai treated her servant shamefully. Overwhelmed and hurt, Hagar fled the impossible situation.

I've felt like running a few times. Have you? But I know God sees what's happening in my life. I also know that if I'll stop and listen with an open heart, I will see His way to proceed. The Lord, who parted seas and rained down manna in the desert, is never without guidance for us. And even our mistakes—when placed in divine hands—can work for good.

God who sees, *remind me today that when You look into my life, You see with compassion. You offer answers for my dilemmas, courage for my fears, and peace in my times of turmoil. Thank You, in Jesus' name. Amen.*

Godly Influence

I will establish my covenant as an everlasting covenant between me and you and your descendants after you for the generations to come (Genesis 17:7).

Scripture: **Genesis 17:1-8**
Song: **"Just a Closer Walk with Thee"**

At a family reunion we listened to a reading of Grandma Johnson's testimony, written 150 years earlier. We, her descendants, were deeply moved as we heard of her decision to follow Christ, her anguish over the loss of a child, her husband's year-long illness, and the agonizing decision over whether to stay in Norway or move to America.

Each generation affects the next. When Abram entered into a covenant with God, promising to obey Him, he could hardly comprehend the scope of that decision. God planned to give him countless offspring. Nations would descend from him, and the covenant would endure for all time.

Abram's steady faith-walk, in spite of delays and adversities, stands as a solid example for his offspring. By his resolve to covenant with God, we too—his descendants by faith—will forever reap God's blessings: "If you belong to Christ, then you are Abraham's seed, and heirs according to the promise" (Galatians 3:29).

Remind me, Lord: *the decisions I make today will have lasting consequences. As I choose to follow You, my influence is not lost to future generations. Let those who follow me feel the impact of Your blessing in my family. Through the holy name of Jesus, my Lord and Savior, I pray. Amen.*

Ready with Blessings

As for Ishmael, I have heard you: I will surely bless him; I will make him fruitful and will greatly increase his numbers (Genesis 17:20).

Scripture: **Genesis 17:15-22**
Song: **"Child of Blessing, Child of Promise"**

Our daughter's wedding was a happy occasion, yet I felt a twinge of sadness that day. Our relationship would forever be changed. Now her life would revolve around her husband. She would visit us, but our home was no longer hers. She would establish her own new household.

Abraham must have had mixed emotions when God announced that, in one year, Sarah would bear the covenant child. On one hand, surely Abraham was glad that he'd finally see God's promise fulfilled. On the other hand, he voiced concerns for Ishmael, his beloved 13-year-old by Hagar. No doubt this father and son had developed a strong bond.

So what would become of Ishmael? God would bless him too. And that was all Abraham needed to know. He accepted God's plan and moved on.

No person is insignificant to God; no detail escapes His attention. Let us talk to Him about all those we love, those who may be close at hand or far away. Commit them to His love, for God is ready with His blessings.

Dear Lord, *You care so deeply for me and mine! Continue to shower blessings on those I love and on those I miss today. And thank You for the Scripture that says: "I have heard you." In Christ's name, amen.*

A Heart of Delight

Direct me in the path of your commands, for there I find delight (Psalm 119:35).

Scripture: **Psalm 119:33-40**
Song: **"Joyful, Joyful, We Adore Thee"**

My 5-year-old granddaughter is a wellspring of joy. Her infectious laughter surrounds any activity she enters, whether she's playing house with her dolls or taking on a new role as a bride or special princess. From the minute she enters my door, she flits around the room giggling and dancing, asking the rest of us to join in.

To me, this is the picture of delight. No restraint—only boundless enchantment. When I watch her, I am reminded that God is watching me to see if I am filled with delight in reading His Word, in serving Him, in praising Him. And do others see the wonder in my eyes, my words, and my actions because of God's awesome grace?

These days, my body often wants to take its ease and refresh itself. But even though I am not dancing on the outside, I can still be filled with fascination for God's ways, ever so delighted to be His child.

Lord, *I delight in Your Word. It gives me the strength to face each day and provides the guidance I need to make good decisions. Fill me with immeasurable joy as I hold tightly to Your hand, and create in me an ever-deepening hunger for Your Word. I pray this prayer in the name of Jesus, my marvelous Savior and Lord. Amen.*

September 11–17. **Jeanne Harmon** of Colorado Springs, is a mentor for the Christian Writers Guild. She and her husband, Pat, have two children.

Choosing the Capable

He chose capable men from all Israel and made them leaders of the people (Exodus 18:25).

Scripture: **Exodus 18:13-27**
Song: **"Learning to Lean"**

As an American, I have the distinct privilege of voting for the men and women of my choice to act as public servants. This right was given to me by the Constitution of the United States, and as a resident of a democratic country, I play a part in choosing who will govern me. This is a daunting responsibility for us citizens.

Since every candidate claims to be the best person for the job, how can we decide? After all, in our day of modern technology, we receive news reports claiming to have the truth about the candidates, but it seems that so little remains completely unbiased. Ultimately, we must rely on our own resources to check a candidate's voting record on the issues and learn all we can about his or her character.

The responsibility of choosing is left to us, just as Moses was allowed to choose the leaders he deemed capable. As we pray and seek God's guidance *about* our leaders, let's remember that He also asks us to pray *for* our leaders, whoever is chosen.

Dear Lord, *often I take for granted the rights and privileges given to me as a citizen. Never let me forget the sacrifices that have been made on my behalf. Remind me to seek after You as my guide and to vote for capable people to govern me. I pray in Jesus' holy name. Amen.*

The Blessing of Obedience

If you obey me fully and keep my covenant, then out of all nations you will be my treasured possession (Exodus 19:5).

Scripture: **Exodus 19:1-9a**
Song: **"I Have Decided to Follow Jesus"**

Dan found that raising a teenager in today's world was harder than he'd once assumed. Efforts to reach out to his son Josh met with resistance. Arguments over clothes, music, curfew, and friends seemed unending. Dan's overtures only made his son run in the other direction. "I make my own choices," Josh said, "so leave me alone."

How Dan longed for a loving relationship with his son! He dreamed of sharing all the good things a father has to give. He wanted to shower Josh with rewards for respect and obedience. This was not to be. Even though Dan loved him, Josh's continual disobedience drove a wedge into their relationship.

Regretfully, we are sometimes like this with our heavenly Father. We pray for guidance, feel the tug in our hearts, and then fail to act. What blessings we give up!

Perhaps it is our fear, our need for security that keeps us in such a state of struggle. Yet God treasures us and our fellowship. And when it comes to security, I am reminded of some good words a missionary once spoke to me: "The hand that *points* the way is the same hand that *provides* the way." What greater safety than that?

Lord, *help me remember today that obeying You leads to blessing and peace. Guide me, and I will follow. Through Christ I pray. Amen.*

Discern and Follow

Direct my footsteps according to your word; let no sin rule over me (Psalm 119:133).

Scripture: **Exodus 19:9b-15**
Song: **"Footprints of Jesus"**

Moses received specific directions from the Lord about how to approach God. He followed, and he serves as a good example for us. In contrast, King Saul, failed to follow.

Before Saul went to battle the Philistines, he took things into his own hands and offered a sacrifice to the Lord without waiting for Samuel to do it. So God took the kingdom from Saul and gave it to David. For Saul, how to respond to following directions was the key to a smashing success . . . or total failure. Psalm-writer David must have known this, for he called out to God: "Direct my footsteps."

Thankfully, God is willing to show us His ways and guide us into His plan. This doesn't mean we will see the future, of course. It simply means determining something crucial in advance: that when we have a choice to make, we will make it according to every bit of heavenly guidance discernible. As Christian apologist C. S. Lewis put it: "Total renunciation can only mean a total readiness for every *particular* renunciation that may be demanded." Your very next decision, then, is quite important.

Father, *my will is to do Your will. But I know I can't follow "in general." I will face specific choices at particular times and places. May I be ready! Through Christ, my sovereign Lord, I pray. Amen.*

Commandments of Protection

Great peace have they who love your law, and nothing can make them stumble (Psalm 119:165).

Scripture: **Exodus 20:1-17**
Song: **"Thy Word"**

My husband and I were casually chatting as we forged through the late afternoon traffic. After stopping at an intersection, the car in front of us proceeded forward. Suddenly, from out of nowhere, another car sped into the intersection without slowing. We witnessed screeching tires, flying glass, and spinning automobiles. Confusion erupted, and soon ambulances rushed to the scene.

Whenever someone breaks the law, it affects more than just that individual. In this case, a man suffered a severe back injury because of another's irresponsibility. In fact, the accident affected everyone involved—families, friends, even the witnesses.

God gave Moses the Commandments so that people could live in right relationship with their creator and with their fellow human beings. That's why the psalmist could speak of *loving* God's law. Those rules—and all their societal derivatives—are clearly for our own good. They protect us against sin and destruction. And the rewards of keeping them are simply out of this world.

Dear Heavenly Father, *I know that keeping Your laws can't save me. But because of Your great and gracious salvation, I can strive to obey You out of love and gratitude. Thank You for giving me peace as I give up sin. In the name of Your Son, my Savior, I pray. Amen.*

Keep Pedaling

We will do everything the Lord has said; we will obey (Exodus 24:7).

Scripture: **Exodus 24:3-8**
Song: **"Be Glorified"**

This guy can ride a bicycle! As the most celebrated contributor to the sport of cycling, Lance Armstrong is a two-time Olympian and a five-time winner of the Tour de France. None of these honors came without significant sacrifice and some cruel setbacks.

In 1996, Lance experienced excruciating pain, and tests revealed cancer that had spread to his brain and lungs. The news stunned the world. Doctors said his chances of survival were less than 50-50. Frightened but determined, Lance took aggressive measures to fight his cancer. Two years later, he had achieved a remarkable recovery and once again challenged the world's bicyclists in competition. As of this writing, he says his cancer experience was a wake-up call that led him to be a spokesman for cancer research.

At times in this race of life I want to give up. In my pain I wonder, "How can I persevere?" At those times I'm reminded of my deep-down commitment to the Lord. In happier times I have often echoed the words of the ancient Israelites: I will obey. Now I recall the motto of Lance Armstrong: Despite the odds, don't quit.

Dear Father, *help me face today's circumstances with confidence, knowing that You are in control. In the name of Jesus I pray. Amen.*

September 17

Savor the Solitude

Moses entered the cloud as he went on up the mountain. And he stayed on the mountain forty days and forty nights (Exodus 24:18).

Scripture: **Exodus 24:12-18**
Song: **"Go Tell It on the Mountain"**

Sarah looked forward to the women's retreat every fall. Ladies from several churches would gather at a campground to worship and hear from God. Silent moments alone with the Lord refreshed Sarah every morning, and she loved singing praises in the solitude of the forest.

She relished escaping her world of e-mailing, car pooling, grocery shopping, and cell-phoning as she spent time in prayer and the Word. Then, leaving the retreat, she was ready to face another year with a renewed spirit.

When she reached home, Sarah nearly burst with joy upon sharing every moment with her husband. He listened patiently, but something was lost in the retelling. Later, in prayer, Sarah sensed the Lord's whisper: "Some things are meant for the secret places You and I share."

I think Moses must have reveled in his 40-day mountain getaway with the Lord, just as Sarah so enjoyed her own retreat. Both were involved in serious business with God, and both would extend their blessings to others. Yet when God meets us, He meets each of us as an individual, beloved child. Do savor that one-to-one relationship.

***Father,** help me find time today to go to the mountain and commune with You. Thank You for wanting me. In Jesus' name, amen.*

Zapping the Joy Killers

Restore to me the joy of your salvation and grant me a willing spirit, to sustain me (Psalm 51:12).

Scripture: **Psalm 51:1-12**
Song: **"Joy to the World"**

Have you noticed that to-do lists can be joy killers? I looked at my list one Saturday morning and wanted to crawl back into bed rather than face the day ahead. I had committed to hosting a dinner at my house that evening. But after an exhausting week, the last thing I wanted to do was to clean house, shop for groceries, and prepare a meal for 12 adults I barely knew.

Tasks on a list aren't the only thieves of joy in life. Boredom, worry, anger, hurt, regret, and exhaustion move us into gloom and even take our eyes away from God. For the psalmist, sin sat at the top of the joy-killer list. Only confession would restore David's zest for life.

Are there joy killers in your life these days? When we ask God to restore our joy, He often takes us to the source of our joy killer. As difficult as it may be, when we face that thing squarely, we've taken the first step toward spiritual renewal. The Lord restored my joy on that Saturday by reminding me of the purpose of my to-do list: to minister to potential new friends through heartfelt hospitality.

Father, *zap any joy killers in my life by helping me confront their source. In the name of Your Son, my Savior, I pray. Amen.*

September 18–24. **Jane Hampton Cook,** author and speaker, is the former White House Deputy Director of Internet News Services for President George W. Bush.

Oldies but Goodies

Write down for yourselves this song and teach it to the Israelites and have them sing it, so that it may be a witness for me against them (Deuteronomy 31:19).

Scripture: **Deuteronomy 31:14-23**
Song: **"There's a Glad New Song"**

"Was that song before your time?" my older husband often asks me when we hear an oldie-but-goodie on the radio or in a restaurant. He enjoys being reminded of an earlier time as the tune conjures good memories of the past. A simple tune can place us in a time warp, taking us back to a more sentimental season in our lives.

God commanded a dying Moses to teach the Israelites a song about His covenant with them. The emotional power of music would help keep His promise alive among the Israelites in the years to come after Moses was gone. It's as if the Lord was the author of the very first oldie-but-goodie.

How has God used music in your life? Does a favorite hymn or praise song draw you to Him as soon as you hear it or sing it? God created music to connect us to Him quickly and emotionally. As He did in the lives of the Israelites, He still uses hymns and spiritual songs to speak to the deepest places of our souls.

Heavenly Father, *thank You for the gift of music. I lift my voice to You in praise and worship. Send me a new song today or use an oldie to remind me of Your love for me through Your covenant in Christ. For it's in His matchless name that I pray. Amen.*

My Hero!

Have I not commanded you? Be strong and courageous. Do not be terrified; do not be discouraged, for the Lord your God will be with you wherever you go (Joshua 1:9).

Scripture: **Joshua 1:1-9**
Song: **"Surely the Presence of the Lord Is in This Place"**

Five years ago today President George W. Bush spoke to the American people and the world by addressing a joint session of Congress following the September 11 terrorism attacks. He uttered six simple words that described my heart at the time: "Freedom and fear are at war." Like many Americans, I found myself afraid to go to work after the attacks. I was also a bit jumpy in other circumstances, such as when the lights suddenly went out during a church service, or whenever I stepped into a subway car.

The Israelites faced a war of freedom versus fear as well. They longed for freedom, but they feared the dangers keeping them from the promised land. So the Lord asked them to be strong and courageous. He didn't guarantee a safe journey, but He promised to be with them amid any dangers they encountered.

You and I hear of tragedies every day. We cannot watch the news on television without observing another incarnation of violence. Yet God calls us to approach life with courage and rest on His promised presence. He is our warrior hero when freedom and fear fight within us.

Dear Lord, *may I rest in Your freedom instead of living in my fear. Thank You for Your promise to be with me always. In Jesus' name, amen.*

Living in the Desert?

Then you lived in the desert for a long time (Joshua 24:7).

Scripture: **Joshua 24:1-7**
Song: **"Shall We Gather at the River?"**

Deserts are sandy, desolate, and wild. They are dry and waterless, burning hot during the day and bone-chilling at night. We may not live there geographically, but sometimes we find ourselves in a desert of spirit. Jobs become stale, finances evaporate, friends disappoint us, and marriages lose their intimacy.

My desert place? Graduate school. I knew God had clearly placed me there—but the dryness I encountered! My finances dipped lower than ever, and my hope for a prosperous career dissolved as I encountered hostility toward my faith from professors and fellow students.

My desert lasted less than four years, but the Israelites lived in the wild for much longer. After experiencing God's miracles and escaping from Egypt, they lived in a barren land that forced them to cry out to God frequently. He heard them and supplied their needs.

The beauty of landing in any desert is God's provision, His ability to sparkle above the sand and grit. Although they lived in the desert for 40 years, the Israelites didn't live there forever. Just as the Lord delivered them, so He will deliver us from our times of desolation.

***O Lord,** thank You for the desert, for its rugged beauty, and for Your sustenance when I enter it. And thank You for Your eternal river of life that cleanses me and refreshes my spirit. In the name of Christ I pray. Amen.*

Inherited Blessing

I gave you a land on which you did not toil and cities you did not build; and you live in them and eat from vineyards and olive groves that you did not plant (Joshua 24:13).

Scripture: **Joshua 24:8-13**
Song: **"Faith of Our Fathers"**

When did you last buy something new? There is something special about the smell of a brand-new car, the crispness of a new shirt, or the clarity of a new cell phone. A feeling of excitement and enthusiasm sweeps over us when something in our life is "the latest thing."

We often measure an item's worth based on its newness. But Joshua 24:13 reveals that God also values what already exists. He reminded the Israelites that their blessings resided in what they had inherited. They lived in cities they did not build and ate from vineyards they did not plant. The old was just as much a blessing as the new.

We have received a rich inheritance. So many of our blessings flow from the work of those who have gone before us. Colonists established townships that are now thriving cities. Inventions, such as Henry Ford's automobile and Thomas Edison's lightbulb, transformed society into the mobile world of communication we enjoy today. Our lifestyle—our inheritance—is as much a blessing as the new things in life. Let us appreciate the past and those who walked before us.

***Lord,** today may I value the old along with the new. And help me leave a legacy of faith to those who will come after me. In Jesus' name, amen.*

Leading by Example

As for me and my household, we will serve the Lord (Joshua 24:15).

Scripture: **Joshua 24:14-18**
Song: **"The Family of God"**

Children are great imitators, often learning by watching adult behavior. When I spent several days with a friend and her six-month-old son, I could easily get Jackson to smile at me just by looking into his eyes and curling up the corners of my mouth. Within seconds his cheeks dimpled into the cutest grin.

As children grow, they continue to imitate their parents in many ways. Even as young adults they often make choices based on parental modeling through the years.

Joshua's words about serving the Lord were credible because he lived them before his followers. When he called on the Israelites to choose whether or not to serve the Lord, he didn't coerce them into it. Instead, he provided a practical model of obedience for them to imitate.

Whether we realize it or not, we serve as models for those around us, especially the youth who are looking on. We have a great opportunity to lead by example. Our words and actions, if compatible, will powerfully influence the coming generation. What a privilege is ours!

Heavenly Father, *show me how to lead by example today. Reveal where I need to change so others may follow not just my words, but my behavior. Thank You that You sent Your Son, Jesus, as the great model, whom I can imitate. I pray in His precious name. Amen.*

Serving, Step by Step

Joshua said, "You are witnesses against yourselves that you have chosen to serve the Lord." "Yes, we are witnesses," they replied (Joshua 24:22).

Scripture: **Joshua 24:19-24**
Song: **"I Would Be True"**

Witnesses are a crucial component of our legal system. They provide accountability in transactions. Attorneys call witnesses to the stand to testify about a case. Marriage licenses, wills, and mortgage contracts require witnesses. But to be credible and effective, they must be truthful.

The Israelites sealed with the oath of witnesses their commitment to serve the Lord. As Joshua banged the gavel, the people agreed to serve the Lord. They also agreed to serve as their neighbors' witnesses.

God didn't need witnesses to know the true intention of their hearts, of course. But they themselves needed the accountability. By public declaration, the Israelites made themselves answerable to their families and communities.

I'm thankful that my service to the Lord is a commitment sealed by the deposition of my own heart. And God serves as both my witness and judge. He knows when my testimony is reliable and honest. He also offers forgiveness when I fail. That is such a good thing because so often my journey down the path of service proceeds with two steps forward and one step back. How is it with you?

Father, *may I be a reliable servant and witness for You. Search my heart and show me where I need to change or improve. Through Christ, amen.*

Son, It's the Law!

Talk about them when you sit at home and when you walk along the road, when you lie down and when you get up (Deuteronomy 6:7).

Scripture: **Deuteronomy 6:4-9**
Song: **"The Law of God Is Good and Wise"**

As a former state trooper, my father wanted to make sure that I knew all the rules of the road as I prepared to take my driver's license exam. He would drill me at night. He would quiz me in the car. He would create scenarios and have me explain what I should do. Road signs, speed limits, safety rules—he covered them all. Eventually I knew I could handle any question on that test.

Many people find it hard to observe laws and rules. Too restrictive! Thus our prisons teem with people who are paying for their limitless "freedom."

Shall we take God's commandments less seriously than we take our society's laws? Hardly! Just as Moses urged the Israelites to continually observe God's laws and to make sure their families knew them well, our families need to know and follow God's commandments. Thankfully, the one who kept all the commandments perfectly tells us: "My yoke is easy and my burden is light" (Matthew 11:30).

***God,** may I see Your commandments not as shackles but as opportunities to show my gratitude for Your salvation. Through Christ my Savior, amen.*

September 25–30. **Jeff Friend** is a speaker and freelance writer living in Largo, Florida, with his wife, Nancy. He is a big fan of the Baltimore Orioles.

Stories for the Ages

We will tell the next generation the praiseworthy deeds of the Lord, his power, and the wonders he has done (Psalm 78:4).

Scripture: **Psalm 78:1-8**
Song: **"Life in the Loon"**

As we walked through the Baseball Hall of Fame in Cooperstown, New York, my father pointed out various bats, uniforms, gloves, and other items on display. He told my brothers and me little stories about some of the great players who had used that equipment in earlier years. Though the names were unfamiliar to me at the time, my father had vivid memories of many of those men, and he enjoyed retelling their historic accomplishments. Other players he knew about from accounts he'd read or heard from others as he was growing up.

Countless museums around the world preserve memories and mementos. By understanding the past—in cultures, sports, art, and myriad other areas—we can relate it to our own lives (and better prepare for the future).

How much more important to tell our children and grandchildren how God has protected and provided for His people down through the generations! We need to share with them His faithfulness, love, and mercy toward us. Then they will know God can be trusted to lead them through whatever they may face.

Heavenly Father, *may I joyfully share the stories of Your faithfulness to me so I can encourage others to follow You. I pray this prayer in the name of Jesus, my praiseworthy Savior and Lord. Amen.*

Slow Down and Listen

I am listening carefully to all the Lord is saying—for he speaks peace to his people, his saints, if they will only stop their sinning (Psalm 85:8, *The Living Bible*).

Scripture: **Psalm 85:4-13**
Song: **"Softly and Tenderly"**

The irate customer ranted at the man behind the counter. She opened the box, yanked out the small appliance, and began waving it in the clerk's face. He tried to interrupt her, but she refused to give him an opening. She just continued to voice her displeasure with the product—and the store in general.

Again the man tried to ask a question, but he was rudely cut off. Then, as another outburst finally subsided, the employee saw his opportunity. "Ma'am, I understand that you are very upset," he said. "But I'm still not sure what is wrong with the product. All I want to do is help you get satisfaction, so please just calm down so we can resolve this." Having been disarmed by the employee's quiet demeanor, the woman apologized and explained the problem. If she'd been willing to listen to him earlier, she could have avoided such an embarrassing confrontation.

When God talks to us, let us listen carefully instead of plunging ahead with any self-centered plans. Hearing Him speak will bring peace to our lives as no other voice can.

Lord, *in my busy world it's easy to let Your voice be overwhelmed by all the noise around me. Help me slow down and listen. In Christ's name, amen.*

Legitimate Shame

Yet you have disobeyed me. Why have you done this? (Judges 2:2).

Scripture: **Judges 2:1-5**
Song: **"O How Happy Are They Who the Savior Obey"**

Why? The question expresses our desire to understand, often when we seem confused and overwhelmed. The dying patient asks, "*Why* did I get this disease?" The laid-off worker asks, "*Why* did I lose my job?" The rejected spouse asks, "*Why* did she walk out on me?" All of us know the feeling of despair that so often accompanies a "why?" But does God know too?

I remember when my parents had warned me, over and over again, not to do something—but I did it anyway through sheer teenage rebellion. I can still recall that look of frustration and disappointment on their faces as they asked, "*Why* did you disobey us?" Then, even though they loved me, they needed to show me that disobedience carries a price to pay.

God also knows about children who disobey. He had instructed the Israelites to tear down the altars of false gods, but they didn't do it. Since they had broken the covenant, they faced God's judgment. But they also had to hear those anguished, pleading words that bring legitimate—and potentially healing—shame to a child: "Why have you done this?"

***God,** I know that obeying You is the way to glorify Your name. May I do Your will with gladness and singleness of heart today. In Jesus' name, amen.*

Keep Telling It

After that whole generation had been gathered to their fathers, another generation grew up, who knew neither the Lord nor what he had done for Israel (Judges 2:10).

Scripture: **Judges 2:6-10**
Song: **"Someone Must Tell the Glad Story"**

When my brother decided to research our family tree, he spent hours scanning genealogy books. He mailed several letters to various agencies, requesting copies of birth and death certificates, marriage licenses, land records, and anything else he thought might help him piece together our family's past. He also interviewed relatives near and far to dig up anecdotes about our ancestors.

I thought his project was a big waste of time. Why should I care about somebody who lived decades before I was born? But then I began wondering whether there might be some things from my forefathers' lives that could instruct me. Were there perhaps certain traditions or beliefs that should not be discarded so lightly?

The Israelites suffered the consequences of ignorance about their ancestors. An entire generation grew up without knowing the Lord or His great works among earlier generations. How sad that they would end up repeating many of their fathers' mistakes, simply because they didn't know how to follow and trust God.

***God,** help me commit to telling the next generation about Your faithfulness and all the great things You have done for me. Our young people need to know that You are able to do the same for them today. In Jesus' name, amen.*

Avoid the Miserable Misery

The Lord had warned Israel he would do this, and now the Israelites were miserable (Judges 2:15, *Contemporary English Version*).

Scripture: **Judges 2:11-15**
Song: **"Draw Me Closer, Lord"**

Stop signs. Medicine labels. Flashing lights. Every day we see warnings of various kinds. Some are obvious and shout at us: Caution! Danger! Do Not Enter! Others may be more subtle, like Fasten Your Seatbelt. But all warnings have one thing in common: they try to keep us safe from some form of danger. If we don't do what the warning says, we may have to deal with some unpleasant consequences.

Disregarding a policeman's warning may get us arrested. Ignoring a medication label may lead to painful side-effects. Laughing off our employer's caution may end in unemployment. But it is always up to us to choose whether to heed a warning.

God's warnings intend to keep us from making decisions that may damage our souls or displease Him. He knows of the dangers that lie ahead in our paths. By reading His Word and listening when He speaks to our hearts, we can count on our Father to guide us into lives of integrity. We won't avoid all danger, of course. But we will no doubt save ourselves significant misery.

Dear Father, *because of Your great love for me, You warn of dangers ahead. How can I ever thank You enough? Through Christ I pray. Amen.*

My Prayer Notes

DEVOTIONS®

***I*n the morning, O Lord, you hear my voice; in the morning I lay my requests before you and wait in expectation.**

—Psalm 5:3

OCTOBER

Photo © Artville

Gary Allen, Editor

Can You Hold, Sir?

I will use [the nations] to test Israel and see whether they will keep the way of the LORD and walk in it as their forefathers did (Judges 2:22).

Scripture: **Judges 2:16-23**
Song: **"Wait, O My Soul, Thy Maker's Will"**

"Thank you for calling. Please wait for the next available representative." As the soft music began playing in my ear, I felt like slamming the telephone down in protest. They want me to wait? *I'm busy!* But this company was the only one that had the data I needed. If I hung up now, I would just have to call back some other time. So I decided to wait it out. . . .

I often find it difficult to wait. It's hard not to have any control over a situation, to want something right away but, for reasons I may not know, to have it withheld.

In the days of the judges, the Lord did not drive out some nations from Israel because He wanted to test His peoples' devotion to Him. Surely the people pleaded for deliverance . . . but the Lord let them wait.

When God doesn't act on our prayers right away, we must believe that He has a reason. Are we willing to trust His wisdom? He does hear, and He *always* answers: sometimes "Yes," sometimes "No," and sometimes "Wait."

Dear God in Heaven, *help me remember that Your timing and Your ways are far wiser than mine. All praise to You, through Jesus Christ, amen.*

October 1. **Jeff Friend** is a speaker and freelance writer living in Largo, Florida, with his wife, Nancy. He is a big fan of the Baltimore Orioles.

Our True Shelter

He that dwelleth in the secret place of the Most High shall abide under the shadow of the Almighty (Psalm 91:1, *King James Version*).

Scripture: **Psalm 91**
Song: **"Hiding in Thee"**

Four cottonwood trees continue to cast their shadows over the South Dakota prairie as they have for more than 100 years. Author Laura Ingalls Wilder's father, Charles Ingalls, planted one for each of his daughters, marking off his homestead claim. The trees provided shady protection in the summer and shelter from pelting snow in the winter. Any home tucked beneath a tree's shadows is safer than one more exposed to the elements.

Yet life itself exposes us to many elements we'd rather not face. A row of trees can't protect us from job layoffs, sicknesses, broken relationships, and other problems.

But God promises to be with us in trouble. Living under His shadow, we are held secure in His love. When we feel we are under attack, God's protective presence is there.

The Ingalls' homestead is long gone, but Pa's cottonwoods remain. Our problems come and go, but God, our loving protector, remains with us forever.

Great Protector, *help me turn to You with full confidence that You are more powerful than any of my problems. Thank You, in Jesus' name. Amen.*

October 2–8. **Jane Heitman** is a library technician living in Grand Junction, Colorado. Among other works, she has authored two books for school librarians.

Spiritual Muscles: Toned Up?

The LORD is my light and my salvation; whom shall I fear? The Lord is the strength of my life; of whom shall I be afraid? (Psalm 27:1, *King James Version*).

Scripture: **Psalm 27:1-6**
Song: **"Shouting His Praise"**

A young couple relaxes under an umbrella at the beach. Just as they get comfortable, a bully appears and kicks sand in the young man's face. The humiliated youth is too weak to defend himself.

This 1930s advertisement promoted an exercise system designed to strengthen a man's muscles so he'd never need to fear bullies. But we believers have something much more potent than any exercise system. The Lord himself gives us strength and salvation. He has already conquered sin and death through Jesus' death and resurrection. So no matter what battles we face, or who our enemies are, the almighty Lord is with us. Yes, we will have trouble in this sinful world, but God is stronger than any trouble. We can face our enemies confidently, knowing that God fights with us and for us.

An exercise system can build strong muscles for a fight with bullies. But exercising spiritual disciplines, such as prayer and Bible study, prepares us for a daily battle of cosmic proportions (see Ephesians 6:12). How is your muscle tone at the moment?

***Lord, my light and salvation,** thank You for fighting my enemies through the victory of the cross. In the name of my victorious Savior, amen.*

Special Delivery

When the children of Israel cried unto the Lord, the Lord raised up a deliverer to the children of Israel, who delivered them, even Othniel the son of Kenaz, Caleb's younger brother (Judges 3:9, *King James Version*).

Scripture: **Judges 3:7-11**
Song: **"Come, Thou Long-Expected Jesus"**

If you must send a package to arrive across the country within two days, you compare shipping companies serving both your area and the destination. You consider which one will get the package where it needs to go, guaranteed on time, for the lowest cost. After you make your choice, you complete the paperwork, and send the package. Then you trust that the company will deliver as promised.

Long ago, the people of Israel trusted God to provide a deliverer. He gave them Othniel, who delivered them from Mesopotamia into a peaceful 40 years. Still, Israel continued to sin. God knew that they—and we—needed more than an earthly deliverer, so when the time was right He sent His Son, Jesus, to offer the perfect, eternal sacrifice for our sins. Jesus' death and resurrection conquered sin forever and delivered forgiveness. And Jesus promises to return to deliver all believers into eternity.

Dear Heavenly Father, *we long for our deliverer as the ancient Israelites did. Unlike them, we know our deliverer is Jesus. Thank You that He will deliver us as promised—on time, guaranteed, with no paperwork, at His cost. Come, Lord Jesus, the one in whom we pray. Amen.*

The Hall of Faith

By [faith] the elders obtained a good report (Hebrews 11:2, *King James Version*).

***Scripture:* Hebrews 11:1, 2, 32-34**
***Song:* "Faith of Our Brothers"**

Family manors frequently have halls lined with portraits of ancestors. A tour through such a home reveals not only the home's current residents but also the generations who built and owned the place down through the years. Though each ancestor is painted to his or her best advantage, his or her *accomplishments* tell the real story. How did each one help build up or tear down the family?

The "hall of faith" described in Hebrews 11 paints pictures of many brave men and women devoted to God. While faith is a gift from God and isn't transmitted genetically or culturally, we can admire these resolute ones as our faith ancestors. When our own faith is flagging, we can be inspired by their perseverance.

Thankfully, we can add to Hebrews' portrait hall of the faithful by naming people in our own lives today who have helped our faith grow. (Whose picture comes to mind right now?) And with God's help, we can live a faithful life so that we too may obtain a good report. Then, next to our portraits in the hall of faith will appear the portraits of those we have encouraged in Christ.

O Lord, *may I be remembered as a builder of Your family through those I've won to You and encouraged in spiritual growth. Thank You for the biblical accounts of the faithful who inspire me. Through Christ I pray. Amen.*

Can You Go Alone?

Barak said unto her, If thou wilt go with me, then I will go: but if thou wilt not go with me, then I will not go (Judges 4:8, *King James Version*).

Scripture: **Judges 4:1-10**
Song: **"Alone with God"**

Two high school students trying to decide their futures consulted with a U.S. Marine recruiter. Fearful of leaving their small town alone, they enlisted under the buddy program, which guaranteed they would be together at least through basic training. They were proud of their decision and exemplified the Marines' motto, *Semper Fidelis,* which is Latin for "always faithful."

In the Bible, Deborah told Barak that God commanded him to enter battle—with a guarantee of victory. God did not command Deborah to go along, but Barak refused to go without her. We don't know why he didn't trust and obey God, but we might guess he was simply afraid. Deborah went along, but told Barak that he would not receive honor for the victory.

Sometimes God gives us buddies to help us face our trials. At other times He wants us to walk forward without human escorts. Either way, God is always faithful; He fulfills His promises. And no matter the earthly outcome, He remains in charge.

God, *I know You want what's best for me, so give me the courage to face daily battles in fellowship with others—or even alone. And thank You so much for always keeping Your promises. I pray in Jesus' holy name. Amen.*

All in Good Time

Deborah said unto Barak, Up; for this is the day in which the Lord hath delivered Sisera into thine hand: is not the Lord gone out before thee? So Barak went down from mount Tabor, [with] ten thousand men (Judges 4:14, *King James Version*).

Scripture: **Judges 4:12-16**
Song: **"Guide Me Ever, Great Redeemer"**

Timing is everything. Tenths of seconds make an Olympic athlete a winner. Seconds taken to administer emergency medical treatment can determine life or death. In minutes, flames can turn buildings to ashes. Timing was everything for Barak too. God told Deborah, His judge over Israel, the right time for Barak to fight Sisera. Barak acted then, and God gave him success.

I've noticed that God's idea of perfect timing rarely matches my own. I often want to charge ahead with an imperfect plan, eager to see results. I may procrastinate to avoid an unpleasant task, making it even more burdensome later. Or I shun service out of sheer laziness, and a wonderful opportunity slips by. Because I cannot see God's *entire* plan, I act blindly unless I allow God to guide me. Deborah recognized the right time because the Lord was with her.

God is also with us! He loves us and wants what is best for us. What would happen if we turned all our impatience, fear, and lethargy over to Him right now?

Eternal God, *today make Your plans my plans. Replace my impatience and apathy with courage and energy. Thank You, in Jesus' name. Amen.*

A Magnifying Melody

Hear, O ye kings; give ear, O ye princes; I, even I, will sing unto the Lord; I will sing praise to the Lord God of Israel (Judges 5:3, *King James Version*).

Scripture: **Judges 5:1-12**
Song: **"Sing, My Tongue, the Glorious Battle"**

Early in the morning, while New Yorkers scurry to work, a garbage collector goes about his job. He heaves smelly, dirty trash into his truck, singing as he goes. Show tunes, pop tunes, standards, arias—he sings whatever strikes him at the moment. Passersby smile and wave. Some call out requests or shout, "Good morning!"

A song can powerfully affect both singer and hearer. Deborah's song sprang from her heart, a hymn full of thanks that magnified the Lord. He had dramatically freed Israel from an oppressive king, and Deborah just had to burst forth in melody. Her song recounts Israel's history in the events leading up to, and including, the enemy's defeat. Anyone listening would know the whole story and join in praising God for deliverance.

Our songs and hymns of praise move our focus from the "trash" in our lives and remind us of the greatness of the king we serve. What hymn can we sing in praise to God today? What song do those around us need to hear?

Dear Lord, *You delivered Your people from enemies time and again. Thank You for delivering us from the ultimate enemy, death, through Your Son, Jesus. Let our songs humble us and glorify You. Help us sing loudly and clearly so that others may come to know You too. In Christ's name, amen.*

Watch for the Goodness

Devote yourselves to prayer, being watchful and thankful (Colossians 4:2).

Scripture: **Colossians 4:2-6**
Song: **"Prayer Is the Soul's Sincere Desire"**

Jim and Kathy have been married for 20 years. They are devoted to each other. Tom is devoted to football. Every season he's glued to his television set from the pre-season until the final playoff game.

Devotion is a good thing, as long as it is well placed. There is certainly nothing wrong with being devoted to our spouses or to a relaxing hobby, as long as it does not replace our primary commitment to God Almighty. In Colossians 4:2, Paul calls the church members to devote themselves to prayer. When we take the time to talk to God—and to listen for Him—things change, doors open, chains fall off.

Like breathing, our prayer life can be a rhythmic "in and out, in and out" as we pour out our hearts to God—confessing, adoring, thanking, and asking Him for what we need . . . and then receiving what He has to tell us. In our devotion to knowing God in this way, we can be on the lookout, watchful and thankful, for His goodness in our lives and in the lives of those for whom we pray.

O Lord, *deepen my commitment to You, and increase my devotion to communicating with You through prayer. In Jesus' name, amen.*

October 9–15. **Jackie M. Johnson** is a freelance marketing writer and creative writer. She has written articles, poetry, and hundreds of devotionals.

Honoring the Hours?

My times are in your hands; deliver me from my enemies and from those who pursue me (Psalm 31:15).

Scripture: **Psalm 31:14-24**
Song: **"Time, by Moments, Steals Away"**

How much is a basketball worth? A basketball in my hands—or yours—is worth about $20. In the hands of NBA superstar Shaquille O'Neal, it's worth quite a few million. Why? Because he is one of the best players in NBA history, and I am . . . *not.*

Psalm 31 tells us that our times are in God's hands. When God is the center of our lives, we can give Him our cares and concerns and trust that He will take care of them, time after time. In His hands, my time is absolutely precious. In my hands, time can be wasted and become virtually valueless.

The challenge, then, is to place ourselves in God's hands at all times—the good and bad times, the exciting and boring times. As novelist Susan Ertz once said: "Millions long for immortality who do not know what to do with themselves on a rainy Sunday afternoon." God knows what to do with our times. He has plans for us, work for us to do in His kingdom. If we will lift up our hearts to Him for direction and protection from enemies, He will surely guide us safely into service.

***O Lord,** how wasteful of precious time I can be! You have given me a limited number of days upon this earth, so let me use them wisely and productively in Your service. In the name of Your Son, my Savior, I pray. Amen.*

Power of Promises Kept

I prayed for this child, and the Lord has granted me what I asked of him. So now I give him to the Lord (1 Samuel 1:27, 28).

Scripture: **1 Samuel 1:21-28**
Song: **"Precious Promise"**

"I promise to love, honor, and obey," said the woman to her groom, and they divorced five years later. "I promise to cut taxes and grow the economy, "said the politician to his supporters, and he didn't do either. Sometimes even our friends and neighbors disappoint us. "Sure, I'll come to your party," someone may say, and then never show up. Why is it so hard for some people to keep their promises?

Hannah wasn't one of those people. She had prayed fervently for a child, vowing that if God would give her a son, then she would give the boy back to Him for full-time service in the temple. When her prayer was finally answered, she kept her promise and took young Samuel to worship and serve God all of his life. God kept His promise to Hannah, and she kept her promise to God.

We serve a promise-keeping God. Therefore, it is a joyful thing to be familiar with all the things He has vowed to do in and among His people. Being aware of His promises, we can depend on them with our whole lives.

Father, *never once have You failed to carry through on Your Word. Today may I depend on You without hesitation. Through Your faithful Son I pray. Amen.*

Rejoice in Your Lord!

Then Hannah prayed and said: "My heart rejoices in the Lord" (1 Samuel 2:1).

Scripture: **1 Samuel 2:1-10**
Song: **"Worship the Lord in the Beauty of Holiness"**

When God answers prayer, the most appropriate response is to worship Him. Hannah did this with emphatic passion. She prayed with fervency and tears for a child of her own, and God granted the request of this barren wife. In return, Hannah poured out her soul in a joy-filled prayer of thankfulness for her miracle.

But how do we know when we are truly worshiping in a way that pleases God? True worship is our sincere, grateful response to God for who He is and what He has done. It is more than singing songs on Sunday morning. It is ascribing worth (adoration, reverence, and respect) to the only one who is truly worthy of our praise. In worship, we acknowledge God's awesome attributes: His character, beauty, majesty, and power. The focus is on God; it's all about Him.

Individuals and nations must carry on the worship of God. Sadly, a 2004 YouGov survey provided overwhelming evidence that the British are now a largely irreligious people, with only 44 percent even believing in God's existence. A tiny minority still attend worship services regularly. Will America soon emulate this once godly people?

Lord, *I adore You. Help me to focus on You and may others see the beauty of your holiness. In Jesus' name, amen.*

Invited to Hear

Eli told Samuel, "Go and lie down, and if he calls you, say, 'Speak, Lord, for your servant is listening'" (1 Samuel 3:9).

Scripture: **1 Samuel 3:1-10**
Song: **"Listen to the Blessed Invitation"**

What if you heard God calling your name, audibly, in the middle of the night? "Mary, Mary!" or "Bob, Bob!" What would you do? That very thing happened to young Samuel in the Old Testament. The boy was sleeping, and the Lord called out his name three different times. When Samuel ran to Eli, his teacher in the temple, with the same "Here I am" reply, Eli realized that it was the Lord calling the boy.

The Lord speaks to us in many ways since Jesus came —through our prayer times, through worship in a song or hymn, through the beauty of creation, and through our intuition. Because of the unfolding progress of revelation, the Old Testament believers literally heard and saw more of God in explicit action. In our day we live by faith, relying on all the wonderful resources God has provided—the Bible, centuries of church history, and His Spirit dwelling within us. Nevertheless, God still longs to reveal His character, His purposes, and His ways; therefore, He still speaks to our hearts in many ways. Whether in ancient or modern days, the key for believers is the same: to listen, to *really* listen—and then respond.

Lord, *I hear You through the Bible, through preaching, through Your Spirit. Help me to listen! In Christ's name, amen.*

Sheer Bliss (from God)

Samuel said to the whole house of Israel, "If you are returning to the Lord with all your hearts, then rid yourselves of the foreign gods and the Ashtoreths and commit yourselves to the Lord and serve him only, and he will deliver you out of the hand of the Philistines" (1 Samuel 7:3).

Scripture: **1 Samuel 7:2-6**
Song: **"Father, Whate'er of Earthly Bliss"**

Marcy enjoyed running, and she was good at it. Every Saturday she would compete in local and regional races and usually bring home a first-place trophy. Soon running became a great love of her life; it was sheer bliss.

No doubt Marcy would second what Eric Liddell (the great 1924 Olympic runner) once said: "I believe God made me for a purpose, but He also made me fast. And when I run, I feel His pleasure."

How wonderful to know deep joy in any pursuit—and to recognize it as a gift from God! Perhaps that is the essence of the difference between praising the creator and somehow idolizing an aspect of His creation. Surely it's what the ancient Israelites often failed to recognize. If only they would take their deep desire to worship—a good thing—and turn it toward the only one who deserved it. Then they would feel His pleasure as well.

Dear Heavenly Father, *I'm thrilled with everything I'm involved in today by Your grace. All good things come from You, and I can only return my thankfulness. Please help me never to forget the source of my joy—You alone! Through Jesus, my deliverer, I pray. Amen.*

Creative Heavenly Aid

While Samuel was sacrificing the burnt offering, the Philistines drew near to engage Israel in battle. But that day the Lord thundered with loud thunder against the Philistines and threw them into such a panic that they were routed before the Israelites (1 Samuel 7:10).

Scripture: **1 Samuel 7:7-13**
Song: **"Spirit of God, That Moved of Old"**

The man was trapped on the roof of his house in a flood, waiting to be rescued while the water overwhelmed the streets below—and kept on rising. A neighbor rowed by in a small boat and offered to rescue him, but the man replied, "I am waiting for God to help me." Next, a helicopter flew overhead, and the pilot asked whether he needed help. Again, same reply.

A silly story, yes. But it makes an important point: when the helping hand of God comes to us, we need to recognize it.

God is surely our helper, but He is also pure spirit (see John 4:24). So He often uses human beings and every form of material, or aspects of nature, to accomplish His purposes. While Samuel was doing the spiritual thing, a thunderstorm routed his enemies. The gracious hand of God alone can save us. But how creative He is in coming to our aid!

O Lord, *my finite mind just can't comprehend the infinite choices available to You in dealing with Your universe. Open my mind to see Your hand at work. Through Your precious Son I pray. Amen.*

Polish Those Nails?

The Lord does not look at the things man looks at. Man looks at the outward appearance, but the Lord looks at the heart (1 Samuel 16:7).

Scripture: **1 Samuel 16:1-13**
Song: **"So Let Our Lips and Lives Express"**

"I always judge a woman by her fingernails," Rick said. I quickly plunged my hands into my pockets. Rick's wife, Sara, has nails that are meticulously manicured, perfectly shaped. My nails are soft, and they chip easily. Obviously.

Sara is slimmer and more outgoing than I am. She is a better cook, a more excellent seamstress, a more prolific writer. Though I had many reasons to compare myself negatively to Sara, I knew I was better at one thing—keeping score: Jean—1, Sara—487.

Sometimes I'm quite thankful that God looks far beneath the surface. But at other times I wish I could touch up the ragged edges of my life with something as simple as a few swipes of an emery board.

"Search me, O God, and know my heart," pleaded the psalmist (139:23). So lately I've given up comparing myself to others. As I stand before my all-knowing God, I want my heart to be free of envy and pride.

Father, *Your Word says I am fearfully and wonderfully made. Help me believe it, no matter whom I meet today. Through Christ, amen.*

October 16–22. **Jean Davis** is a freelance writer who lives in Clarksville, Delaware, with her husband.

Atmosphere of Indwelling

One of the servants answered, "I have seen a son of Jesse of Bethlehem who knows how to play the harp. He is a brave man and a warrior. He speaks well and is a fine-looking man. And the Lord is with him" (1 Samuel 16:18).

Scripture: **1 Samuel 16:14-23**
Song: **"May the Mind of Christ My Savior"**

As a young adult, I couldn't talk about the inner turmoil I felt. I just didn't have the vocabulary to describe my feelings. But every time I visited one family in our church, I left their home feeling better. In their presence, my spirit quieted down. The atmosphere created by their presence—more than their spoken words—gave me peace. I knew the Lord was with them, and I found the comfort of the comforter simply by sitting on their sofa. In time, I found emotional healing as well.

Whatever spirit dwells in us seems to create an atmosphere. So do our words and attitudes. So does music. Though David's music soothed Saul's troubled spirit, surely David's presence did, too, because the Lord was with that young man.

When others come to me, I want God's presence in my life to create an environment that conveys openness, honesty, and love. When others speak of my character or accomplishments, may they say: "The Lord is with her."

Lord God, *when others look at me, I want them to see Your Son, Jesus. May I bring comfort to the hurting by allowing Your comfort to dwell in me. All praise to You, in Christ's name. Amen.*

Credentials, Please!

You are not able to go out against this Philistine and fight him; you are only a boy, and he has been a fighting man from his youth (1 Samuel 17:33).

Scripture: **1 Samuel 17:32-37**
Song: **"Victory All the Time"**

Last week my friend, a high school graduate, met a man who works in the same type of job she has, but for a competitor. After Dr. Somebody introduced himself, he raised one bushy eyebrow and asked, "So, what are your credentials?" Though the invitation to compare her background to his would have rattled her a few years back, my friend now had a ready answer: "Experience."

David knew what he was up against, and he also knew his experience. Was a giant target of a man a more dangerous foe than a bear or a lion—he'd been victorious over them? David was confident that the Lord who had delivered him before would deliver him again.

When we see a door of opportunity open, someone might say we're too young—or too old, too dull, too timid—for the challenge. We may be told we don't have the right education, we're not the right gender or race to get the job done. But if God has prepared us, we'll know we're ready.

Mighty Lord, *when voices of doubt come, bring to my memory Your work in my life so far. And help me remember how You've prepared me for the task at hand. Let me move forward with confidence, boldly proclaiming, "The Lord is with me." I pray through my deliverer, Jesus. Amen.*

Request and Expect

In the morning, O Lord, you hear my voice; in the morning I lay my requests before you and wait in expectation (Psalm 5:3).

Scripture: **Psalm 5**
Song: **"Jesus, Thine All-Victorious Love"**

I know a woman who daily fights the battle of the bulge as she maintains a weight loss of over a hundred pounds. Though she now eats nutritionally and exercises, part of her battle plan is to roll out of bed every morning . . . onto her knees. Each day she humbly asks God for His help with her food choices, emotions, appetites, family, job, and relationships.

Psalm 60:12 says, "With God we will gain the victory." David found the key to victory—praying, then waiting in expectation for the Lord.

I believe we can fight our battles as David fought his. In the morning—every morning—we can lay our requests before God. Yes, the enemies of fear and doubt will press to whisper lies like, "You can't do it; you'll never succeed, so why try?" Even after a colossal failure, we can wait in expectation for Him to do for us what we can't do for ourselves. We don't have to fight our battles alone. We can open our lives to God and let His victory become ours.

Dear Father, *thank You for victory in Jesus. May I daily approach Your throne boldly, ever aware of Your great faithfulness as I wait in expectation for You and Your work in my life. In the name of the Father, the Son, and the Holy Spirit, I pray. Amen.*

That's God

David asked, "Where shall I go?" "To Hebron," the Lord answered (2 Samuel 2:1).

Scripture: **2 Samuel 2:1-7**
Song: **"Shepherd, Show Me How to Go"**

My friend Barbara called to say she had several errands to run before we met for lunch. Since she couldn't tell me exactly what time she'd be through, I suggested we meet at one of her stops, the Division of Motor Vehicles.

A strange place to meet, but we soon saw God's hand in our decision. When Barbara asked to change the address on her license, a clerk told her that their records showed she had no insurance coverage. Though Barbara knew there must be a mistake, the clerk kept her license, and Barbara was stranded—or would have been if God hadn't provided transportation: my car.

OK, it's a small thing. But I believe God cares about each moment of our lives and delights in blessing us with His big and small gifts. With the bigger things—when we need direction in life, as David did—we can ask, and God will answer. At other times, our steps are being ordered by the Lord without our awareness.

While we waited for the return of her license, Barbara said, "Isn't it amazing we chose to meet at the DMV?"

"That's God," I said. "You always say that," she answered. Yes, and there's reason.

***God,** how can I thank You for the care You show me each day? I'm so grateful You enjoy surprising me with Your goodness! Through Christ, amen.*

Humble Beginnings, God's Plan

Now then, tell my servant David, "This is what the Lord Almighty says: I took you from the pasture and from following the flock to be ruler over my people Israel. I have been with you wherever you have gone" (2 Samuel 7:8, 9).

Scripture: **2 Samuel 7:8-17**
Song: **"Little Is Much When God Is in It"**

When Ben Carson was in fifth grade, other students called him Dummy. There were reasons for the taunt. The African-American youngster missed most words on spelling tests and got every math problem wrong. But it didn't matter because God had a plan for Ben. For one thing, his mother saw the potential in all her children. After asking God for direction, she required both her sons to read two books per week and give her written book reports (though Mom couldn't read!). By the middle of sixth grade, Ben moved to the top of his class.

He is now Dr. Ben Carson, director of the Division of Pediatric Neurosurgery at Johns Hopkins, with three best-selling books to his credit. His brother, Curtis, is a successful engineer.

Who would have thought the fifth-grade "dummy" would one day perform brain surgery? Well, who would have thought a boy tending sheep would be king? Yet no matter where we've come from, God has been with us wherever we've gone. He also has our future in view.

Heavenly Father, *You see the beginning and the ending, and with You all things are possible. I praise You through Christ my Lord. Amen.*

Because We Needed It

King David went in and sat before the Lord, and he said: "Who am I, O Sovereign LORD, and what is my family, that you have brought me this far?" (2 Samuel 7:18).

Scripture: **2 Samuel 7:18-29**
Song: **"I Can Only Imagine"**

Ever get discouraged by the little irritations of life? A stubborn hangnail—or an ornery pup that just won't house-train— can certainly get on my nerves. But when I think about Jesus, about God's mercy, grace, and love, about where I am now and where I've come from . . . I find that my mood changes.

Oswald Chambers's March 27 devotional from *My Utmost for His Highest* offers this encouragement: "Compare this week in your spiritual history with the same week last year and see how God has called you up higher." I may look at my performance today and be discouraged, but when I consider how far God has brought me, I am filled with gratitude.

Who are we that God has chosen us? What manner of love is this to be given the privilege of living as children of the most high God? We have done nothing to deserve such mercy and grace. We've *received* it simply because we *needed* it.

Almighty God, *when I think of Your faithfulness over the years, my heart rejoices. How can I be discouraged when I consider Your great love? You are so good! I praise You today through the wonderful name of Your Son, Jesus Christ my Lord. Amen.*

Act, Don't React

He wrote [the proverbs] to teach his people how to live—how to act in every circumstance, for he wanted them to be understanding, just and fair (Proverbs 1:2, 3, *The Living Bible*).

Scripture: **Proverbs 1:1-7**
Song: **"Only a Sinner"**

My 10-year-old daughter's face was ashen. "The substitute teacher thought I took Lindsey's green pencil sharpener," she said, dropping her red book bag to the floor. "She asked me to confess, Mommy," she continued before bursting into tears. "But I *didn't* take it!"

"I'm sure it wasn't you, honey," I said, drawing her close to me. "I feel like calling the principal right now."

"No, it's OK, Mom. You don't have to do anything. We worked it out already," she continued. "After Lindsey cooled down, I told her why I had a green sharpener—that I'd traded my special pencil for Emily's green sharpener over the weekend."

"Well, I'm glad you two worked it out, but I don't like it when my sweet, well-behaved little girl is falsely accused by some uppity stranger who knows nothing about her good character!"

What about your character? my conscience prodded, just after I'd pounded my fist on the kitchen table. . . .

My Lord and King, *when anyone in my family is falsely accused, please help me respond calmly and wisely. In Christ's precious name I pray. Amen.*

October 23–29. **Linda Eckman,** a newspaper reporter and songwriter living in Kennett Square, Pennsylvania, began writing for Christian publications in 1990.

Wisdom: a Treasure Hunt

"It's not here," the oceans say; and the seas reply, "Nor is it here" (Job 28:14, *The Living Bible*).

Scripture: **Job 28:12-28**
Song: **"Teach Me Thy Way, O Lord"**

One of my daughter's favorite pastimes when she was little was to make me a treasure map and have me go scampering throughout the house to find a hidden surprise. "You're not warm at all, Mommy," she beamed on Mother's Day. "Over there, try over there!" she said, pointing behind the couch where a yellow tag was noticeably sticking out.

"Don't give it away yet, silly," I said. "Let me look just a little longer. I like this game, so don't make it so easy!" But finally, after she could contain herself no longer, she proudly handed me a handmade clay jar. "It's a special place to put your rings, Mommy. It's just like your growned-up glass one."

Chrissy had shown me what it meant to search for wisdom. On my own I sometimes find a tiny nugget of truth or just a glimpse of what seems to be wisdom. But if I want to be truly wise, I'll go to where it's "hidden": God's Word. To love and reverence the Lord is to be truly wise. However, we must be as little children to enter in and partake of wisdom's heavenly sweetness.

***Father,** I need wise guidance and encouragement daily. Thank You for providing the teaching and fellowship of the church to help meet this need. But most of all, thank You for Your written Word. In Jesus' name, amen.*

Sweet, or Just Poison?

No, I haven't turned away from what you taught me; your words are sweeter than honey (Psalm 119:102, 103, *The Living Bible*).

Scripture: **Psalm 119:97-104**
Song: **"Sweet, Sweet Spirit"**

I'm a recovering sugar-holic and still crave my daily dose of chocolate. But I've found that honey can be a good alternative for soothing my sweet tooth. On the one hand, sugar is known to pervert our appetites and increase our chances for dental visits, diabetes, and pancreatitis. On the other hand, honey—in moderation—offers the body 15 nutrients and is an excellent food.

Sugar also causes fermentation in the stomach, leading to bacterial growth. But honey, in its raw state, tends to aid digestion. It even acts as a natural antibiotic as it satisfies the appetite and enters the bloodstream slowly.

I'm glad the psalmist likened God's words to honey. The Word brings a sweetness to life that satisfies our longing for rich intimacy. Nothing in our lives is so perfect as God's counsel.

I think it's safe to say that when the psalmist speaks of false teaching, he alludes to words that are nutrient-free. Like sugar, they are empty, non-sustaining, and can even be considered poison to our inner being.

Dear God, *thank You for the gifts You've given me. Keep Your Word flowing in my soul and increase my love for Your Son, Jesus, in whom I pray. Amen.*

This Seat: Reserved!

Then King David said, "Call in Bathsheba." So she came into the king's presence and stood before him" (1 Kings 1:28*)*.

Scripture: **1 Kings 1:28-40**
Song: **"Face to Face"**

No doubt Bathsheba was shaking in her boots when she heard the ominous command, "Come, Bathsheba." This appointment with King David was no small thing. David was now very old, and one of his sons, Adonijah, had suddenly declared himself the next king. However, David had long ago promised Bathsheba that her son, Solomon, would be the next king.

When Bathsheba complained about Adonijah's actions, she simply had to hold her breath and await David's response. Would he remember and fulfill his promise to make Solomon the king after him? Or would David be angry with Bathsheba's nagging?

Yes, if I were Bathsheba, I might be quite nervous. However, David decreed that Solomon would indeed sit upon the kingly throne, just as promised. (Sigh of relief!)

Like Solomon, we've been promised a kingly inheritance: "Those who receive God's abundant provision of grace and of the gift of righteousness [will] reign in life through the one man, Jesus Christ" (Romans 5:17). You see, there is a place of honor already reserved for us.

O God, *in my times of doubt or fear, help me recall Your precious promises to me. They are are so encouraging and uplifting. Thank You! In the name of the Father, the Son, and the Holy Spirit, I pray. Amen.*

Imperfect? Still Ask!

The Lord appeared to him in a dream that night and told him to ask for anything he wanted, and it would be given to him! (1 Kings 3:5, *The Living Bible*).

Scripture: **1 Kings 3:3-9**
Song: **"Yesterday, Today, and Forever"**

Put yourself in Solomon's shoes for a moment and imagine that you're a young adult and almighty God appears to you in a dream. The Lord tells you to ask for anything you want; it will be given to you.

What's amazing to me is that Solomon's wish would be granted, regardless of whether or not he was perfectly following God. First Kings 3:3 reads, "Solomon loved the Lord and followed all of his father David's instructions except that he continued to sacrifice in the hills and to offer incense there"*(TLB)*. The altar at Gibeon is where God appeared to Solomon in the dream—but Gibeon was apparently one of those "hills," a high place of disobedience.

Isn't it interesting that God looked beyond Solomon's imperfections and, with great grace, extended toward him the gift he sought? This problem of weakness and disobedience is something I have in common with Solomon. While I desire to please God in all ways, I fall short of the goal. Yet God—the same yesterday, today, and forever—still provides the gift of His forgiveness and blessing.

Lord of All, *thank You that we can come boldly to Your throne of grace, not because we're good and deserving, but because we're sinners. Praise to You, in the name of Jesus, my merciful Savior and Lord. Amen.*

A Double Dip for Me Too

I will also give you what you didn't ask for—riches and honor! (1 Kings 3:13, *The Living Bible*).

Scripture: **1 Kings 3:10-15**
Song: **"You Can Have a Song in Your Heart"**

I think I've caught King Solomon double dipping. This is one instance that I know of when a Bible character was actually awarded his cake and given permission to eat it too. Not only did God provide Solomon what he asked for (a wiser mind than anyone else's), but He awarded the young king with riches and honor too—things he *didn't* request.

Something like this happened to me recently. You see, four times a year I self-publish a free newspaper and hand-deliver all 7,500 copies throughout my county. My intent is simply to reach people with the good news of Jesus Christ. For the latest issue, God had apparently given me a retired newspaper editor to help me typeset the paper. But when that didn't work out, the paper came to a grinding halt.

Now I needed a particular publishing software, but I just couldn't afford it. So I petitioned God to intervene. He answered—sent me another newspaper lady . . . and . . . brought a computer-whiz stranger to my office. This man handed me (free of charge) exactly—to the T—the publishing software I needed. Talk about a double dip!

Heavenly Father, *thank You for answering my requests, spoken and unspoken. Through Christ, I praise Your holy name! Amen.*

Sands of the Seashore

God gave Solomon wisdom and very great insight, and a breadth of understanding as measureless as the sand on the seashore (1 Kings 4:29).

Scripture: **1 Kings 4:29-34**
Song: **"All Creatures of Our God and King"**

I head to Cape Henlopen in Delaware on a beautiful winter morning. Upon arriving at the eastern shore, my breath is taken away. I am captivated by the beauty of the endless coast, and that first glimpse of God's magnificent ocean always causes my heart to leap for joy.

At the height of the tourist season, I like to watch the children run and play in ankle-deep surf, while others tenaciously build castles in the sand, and numerous adults forget their problems and stress.

I find it amazing that God promised Abraham that his descendants would eventually number more than the sand on the seashore.

The metaphor of sand comes forth in our Scripture passage: Solomon's insight, wisdom, and understanding will be as measureless as the seashore's grains of sand. After reading this passage about Solomon's wisdom, I don't think I will ever be able to look at the millions of particles of loose, opaque grains in the same way. But what analogy could even begin to convey the measureless wisdom of God himself?

O Majestic Father, *thank You for leaving us a visual reminder that Your wisdom is far beyond our comprehension. Through Christ I pray. Amen.*

God, the Under-Appreciated

Great is the LORD and most worthy of praise; his greatness no one can fathom (Psalm 145:3).

Scripture: **Psalm 145:1-7**
Song: **"No Other Name"**

I'd spent over five months preparing an outreach event for some young people so they could minister in schools where I live in France. I poured myself completely into the project, and by the final presentation, I was exhausted in every sense of the term. I was shocked, therefore, when the leader of the speaking groups publicly thanked someone else profusely for . . . hardly doing anything at all.

Later, I thought about how often it must happen to God. He created a paradise for us, complete with beautiful oceans, majestic mountains, countless varieties of wildlife, and a perfect ratio of gases in the air for us to breathe. He even sent His own Son to pay for our sins.

Yet whom do we praise in our upside-down culture today? A movie star who plays wonderful roles but may lack everyday integrity? A billionaire who has stepped on countless people all the way up the ladder? A guy who can jump and put a ball in a basket? Even a minister who preaches powerful sermons? But guess who goes unnoticed, unrecognized, and thoroughly under-appreciated.

***God,** I have no excuse for ignoring Your greatness and worthiness of all praise today. I pause right now and say thanks! Through Christ, amen.*

October 30, 31. **Tim Bennett** is a missionary to France involved in church planting. He has written two books: *With a Grain of Salt* and *Salt for the Supper Table.*

No Grave, Not Yet!

Great is your love toward me; you have delivered me from the depths of the grave (Psalm 86:13).

Scripture: **Psalm 86:8-13**
Song: **"Hear My Cry"**

It's easy to complain when we find ourselves in difficulties. Yet it's in difficulties that we can see the *depths* of God's love (you can't get much lower than a grave).

Have you ever wondered why David was so exuberant in his praise to God? It's easy. He knew that without God's intervention he'd be dead. The problem today is that we don't always see God's protective hand upon us; we fail to recall what He has saved us from (an eternal grave).

There was one time, though, when I saw it very clearly. I was peacefully driving a tiny rental car on wet pavement when it hydroplaned into a guardrail. A van then hit me from behind, and my dented car stopped cold.

I ran to see whether the other driver was OK. He was. I needed my suitcase, so I rushed back to my car . . . just before a semi truck ran over it. Then I heard these lyrics sounding from the still-playing radio: "He didn't bring us this far to leave us." The timing was too perfect. I sang the song for weeks around the house. The kids complained, of course, because of the repetition. But I had a joy that couldn't be quenched. I ignored them and kept singing. Hey, I'd been delivered from the cold earth!

Ever-caring Lord, *I know You've protected me so many times, often without my knowledge. I praise and thank You in Jesus' name. Amen.*

DEVOTIONS®

In you my soul takes refuge. I will take refuge in the shadow of your wings.

—Psalm 57:1

NOVEMBER

Photo © Eyewire

Gary Allen, Editor

Reigning in My Life?

The Lord reigns, he is robed in majesty (Psalm 93:1).

Scripture: **Psalm 93**
Song: **"Awesome God"**

Sixteen-year-old Sarah Huoy crouched under a table in the library at Columbine High School in Littleton, Colorado, on April 20, 1999, as two fully armed teenagers taunted and killed 10 classmates all around her. Not knowing what else to do, she began to pray, "God, send down your angels and make us invisible."

Immediately she felt a peace beyond her understanding. Minutes later she could see the shoes of the killers directly in front of her desk. One of them bumped a chair that hit her. Then, for some reason, the killers hesitated and left the room. This gave Sarah and others precious time to run for safety.

It's unlikely that many of us reading this account will experience such a dramatic confrontation with death as Sarah did. Often we may get the idea, however, that we ought to be able to control our lives quite well; when things aren't going according to our plans, we become anxious. Yet, if we trust that God is truly reigning in our lives, and that He is ultimately in charge, we can be at peace, regardless of the circumstances.

Lord, *You are a God of peace. If I give You all my anxieties, You will take care of all the things troubling me. Thank You, in Jesus' name. Amen.*

November 1–5. **Tim Bennett** is a missionary to France involved in church planting. He has written two books: *With a Grain of Salt* and *Salt for the Supper Table.*

No Satisfaction?

Elijah went before the people and said, "How long will you waver between two opinions? If the Lord is God, follow him; but if Baal is God, follow him" (1 Kings 18:21).

Scripture: **1 Kings 18:17-24**
Song: **"I Belong to Jesus"**

Today, in western countries, worshiping literal idols is a little out of fashion. We do, however, battle the world's way of doing things as opposed to God's way.

As a teenager I had rejected God and tried living virtually without a spiritual life. The world said, "You need a girlfriend to be happy." So I found one. The world said, "Love means you don't need to get married." So we lived together. The world said, "Do your own thing." So I just stopped working, read books, and went to therapy.

My psychologist told me that my problems were actually my parents' fault. Great! But why wasn't I *satisfied* with my life?

Finally, someone challenged me to accept what the Bible had to say about my root problems—pride and rebellion against God. Simply put, that meant I faced a choice: God or the world. No more wavering!

I chose the Lord, and when I entered the waters of baptism—that's when my life started to turn around. That's when the satisfaction started kicking in.

***Lord,** so often I seem to be of two minds. Forgive me for sometimes placing the world's standards above Yours. Empower me by Your Spirit today to live only for Your glory. In Jesus' name I pray. Amen.*

Grateful Doing

Midday passed, and they continued their frantic prophesying until the time for the evening sacrifice. But there was no response, no one answered, no one paid attention (1 Kings 18:29).

Scripture: **1 Kings 18:25-29**
Song: **"All-Consuming Fire"**

How ridiculous those prophets of Baal! They tried everything to please their god but couldn't even attract his attention. It reminds me of a woman whose husband was quite demanding. Every day he would give her a long to-do list. Wanting to please him, she worked as hard as she could to finish all the tasks. But she was never sure whether she did the jobs well enough; she never knew if her work had gained the longed-for acceptance.

One day the husband died. The woman later married a man with whom she was very much in love. He was a different kind of husband and treated her kindly. She was delighted, therefore, to do all she could to return his love. Coming across one of the old to-do lists, she was amazed. She had done all those things that very day, but with a light heart of love rather than fear.

Clearly, the *reason* we serve God makes all the difference. Religion says we *must* do in order to earn God's favor. Christianity says we gratefully *can* do because we already have His full acceptance.

Father, *You love me while I'm a sinner—and You can't possibly love me more than You already do. All praise to You, through Christ Jesus! Amen.*

Keeping the Best?

Elijah said to all the people, "Come here to me." They came to him, and he repaired the altar of the Lord, which was in ruins (1 Kings 18:30).

Scripture: **1 Kings 18:30-35**
Song: **"On Bended Knee"**

At the altar of the Lord, the people of Israel were supposed to sacrifice their best animals and so obtain forgiveness of their sins. But Elijah found this altar in ruins; its function was no longer in vogue. Had the people simply decided to keep "the best" to themselves?

As a believer, I've found one of the hardest things for me to do is to lay my deepest desires and best dreams before God. For some reason I get the idea that I actually know better than God what is best for me. So I hesitate to offer my whole self—all I am and all I have. Yet I know God is waiting for me to lay it all down. That way, He can resurrect it, if it is of Him. Or He can let it die . . . so He can give me something better.

Years ago I sensed God leading me to buy a house. I found the perfect place, made an offer, and then watched it go to someone else. Feeling I'd misread God, I wanted to chuck the whole idea. Instead, God encouraged me (through Hebrews 10:39) not to "shrink back" into unbelief but to continue in faith. He ended up providing a much better house than the one I had set my heart on.

Lord, *You know best what is best for me. Show me the relationship, the dream, the desire that I need to lay before You now. In Jesus' name, amen.*

Time to Pray Aloud?

Answer me, O Lord, answer me, so these people will know that you, O Lord, are God, and that you are turning their hearts back again (1 Kings 18:37).

Scripture: **1 Kings 18:36-39**
Song: **"The Battle Belongs to the Lord"**

As Elijah's battle with the false prophets demonstrates, answered prayer has an amazing way of getting the attention of unbelievers. It can make a real splash!

Notice Elijah's heart in this passage. His motivation was the welfare of the onlookers. He wanted a manifestation of God's power, not so he could be a big shot in town, but so the people would know that God wanted their hearts back. In other words, Elijah already knew how awesome God was. He wanted the people to know too.

Sometimes, however, people are like the prophets of Baal—they aren't ready to be prayed for until they have exhausted all other possibilities. They are convinced they can solve their problems without God. This leaves them in control, and often they have to try everything before becoming desperate enough to let us pray for them.

Are there people in your life who have already tried everything to make life worth living—but still long for more? Perhaps now is the time to pray for them aloud, on purpose, in their presence.

Lord, *show me if there are people in my life right now who are ready for me to offer prayer on their behalf. Give me the boldness to ask them, and to do it, so You can reveal Your love in a tangible way. Through Christ, amen.*

Gone Forever

As far as the east is from the west, so far has he removed our transgressions from us (Psalm 103:12).

Scripture: **Psalm 103:1-12**
Song: **"Sinners, Rejoice: Your Peace Is Made"**

Science tells us that the universe is so vast and complex that even our most powerful telescopes can't measure its dimensions. No matter which direction we look, north, south, east, and west appear to go on forever, never meeting at any point in time or space.

What a great picture of God's forgiveness! When we humbly repent of our sin, He promises to forgive us for each one, every time we ask. The guilt of all our sin—past, present, and future—has been carried away into the wilderness by Jesus, the divine "scapegoat" (see Leviticus 16:7-26), never to return to us.

It boggles the mind to think of anyone offering forgiveness like that. God doesn't continue to bring up our sin once it's confessed. When He forgives, it's over, finished, gone forever. Therefore, let us forget too and move ahead with our lives. As someone once put it: "God buries our sins in the deepest sea and then places a floating sign above the spot. The sign says: No fishing!"

Dear Lord, *when I think of Your forgiving me like this, I'm overwhelmed. I feel alive, loved, and humbled. My guilt and condemnation are gone because of Jesus, the one in whom I pray. Amen.*

November 6–12. **Mabelle Reamer** is a recent graduate of Philadelphia Biblical University, having earned a master's degree in counseling.

November 7

One Turn at a Time

I will instruct you and teach you in the way you should go; I will counsel you and watch over you (Psalm 32:8).

Scripture: **Psalm 32**
Song: **"My Lord Knows the Way Through the Wilderness"**

It was almost 9:00 one Friday evening when my husband received a frantic call from our daughter. After visiting friends at a mall some distance from where we live, she had taken a few wrong turns as she drove home. Now she was lost. My husband, who was familiar with the area, talked her through the confusing exits and road signs until she found a street she knew led home.

Day-to-day problems and pains can be overwhelming, and they often leave us feeling as if we've lost our bearings. In our struggle to find our way through, it's easy to end up disoriented and worried, not knowing what to do next. It seems the more we try to figure things out, the more disoriented we can become.

Of course, God knows exactly where we are, and we don't have to go it alone. He's promised not to leave us floundering by ourselves. We have His promise that He'll go before us and talk us through each confusing, frightening turn, one at a time—until the day we go home to be with Him.

Father, *quiet my heart and mind, and help me find peace in just being with You. Help me to trust You in the turmoil and to remember that You're already present in my tomorrow. So guide me through this day, one moment at a time. In Jesus' name, I pray. Amen.*

Purifying Tears

Rend your heart and not your garments. Return to the Lord your God, for he is gracious and compassionate, slow to anger and abounding in love, and he relents from sending calamity (Joel 2:13).

Scripture: **Joel 2:12-17**
Song: **"Cleanse Me"**

When my children were small, part of their discipline for bad behavior would involve the occasional time-out. They'd have to go upstairs and sit quietly on a chair for a specified time. During one such occasion I sat down with my child to talk about *why* he'd been sent upstairs. He appeared to understand he'd done wrong, and he offered an apology. By all appearances everything went back to normal. I found out later that I'd only succeeded in making him change his outward behavior—not his heart.

Sometimes I secretly enjoy giving the *appearance* of walking closely with God, of saying sincere prayers, and deeply loving all of my fellow church members. It's easier that way, because seeing my heart—as it tends to be most of the time—is painful and humbling. But my gracious and merciful God knows I need to grieve over my heart, which so easily wanders into total self-interest. Is it perhaps only with tears that a heart can be purified?

Heavenly Lord, *I know that my motives are often impure. Forgive me for my deceit and pride. May Your Spirit reveal those things in me that need to change. (I don't like asking this, Lord, because it's hard and it hurts. Give me the courage to do it anyway.) In Jesus' name, amen.*

November 9

Eyes on the Prize

He did what was right in the eyes of the Lord and walked in all the ways of his father David, not turning aside to the right or to the left (2 Kings 22:2).

Scripture: **2 Kings 22:1-7**
Song: **"I Am Resolved"**

My favorite part of the Olympics is watching the sprinters as they scramble toward the finish line. They all strain mightily to receive a gold medal to hang around their necks. They must focus on their goal and not be distracted by the crowd or whomever is running next to them.

It's been said that what has our attention has *us,* and it doesn't take much to pull our eyes away. Loss, disappointment, fear of public opinion—these are only a few of the things that can distract us and keep us from finishing well.

In Old Testament times, King Josiah must have wanted to finish well, determining that nothing would keep him from being the person God wanted him to be. He didn't turn right or left, but headed straight to the finish line.

What would that mean for you or me today? For one thing, moving straight ahead for the Lord will affect our televised entertainment choices. How can we be "right in the eyes of the Lord" when our own eyes are filled with so much that *isn't* quite right?

Father, *I want to run this race as the apostle Paul did—with my eyes always on the prize. Please help me to stay focused on you and finish well! In Jesus' name, amen.*

A Treasure Found

Then Shaphan the secretary informed the king, "Hilkiah the priest has given me a book." And Shaphan read from it in the presence of the king (2 Kings 22:10).

Scripture: **2 Kings 22:8-13**
Song: **"Thy Word"**

There's something about a letter that keeps a person close to us even when they are physically far away. After my father died, I regretted not having any hand-written letters from him to tuck away and reread. So imagine my thrill a few months later when I discovered several letters he'd written to me years earlier. I'd forgotten about them!

Those precious missives were the next best thing to having him with me. They were a special gift that had been lost but found, something I would always treasure.

Somehow in the years before Josiah's reign, the Book of the Law (the first five books of our Bible today) had been lost and forgotten. Imagine the king's excitement at such a find after all the years of not having any writings from God himself.

Scripture overflows with messages from our God to us, with words that will encourage, inspire, and change us as we read them. Are they something we cherish and read over and over? Or are they more like a forgotten, lost treasure waiting to be discovered?

Great God of the Bible, *without Your Word I can't know who You are—or become the person You want me to be. Make Your words so fresh and new in my heart that I'll want to reread them every day. In Jesus' name, amen.*

Personal Influence

The king stood by the pillar and renewed the covenant in the presence of the Lord—to follow the Lord and keep his commands, regulations and decrees with all his heart and all his soul. . . . Then all the people pledged themselves to the covenant (2 Kings 23:3).

Scripture: **2 Kings 23:1-5**
Song: **"I Love You, Lord"**

By adopting the U.S. Constitution and Declaration of Independence, our nation's founders pledged themselves to keeping and protecting for the rest of their lives all that those documents asserted. The example of those men inspired others to take those writings as their own. Many of the early patriots, just ordinary citizens, would give their lives to insure the freedom proclaimed therein. And over 200 years later, we're still influenced by the men who penned the words of those great texts.

In fact, every human extends some form of influence, whether for good or bad. After God's Law had been found, King Josiah stood before the people and pledged to follow it with all his heart and soul, for the rest of his life. His example encouraged all the people to do the same.

You may be just one person, but one way or another you're having an impact on those around you. Be assured, someone is following your example.

***Lord,** thank You for those whose lives have encouraged me to reach for my dreams and to walk closer to You. Help me to provide the same encouragement to every person who looks up to me. Through Christ I pray. Amen.*

Extraordinary Hall of Fame

Neither before nor after Josiah was there a king like him who turned to the Lord as he did—with all his heart and with all his soul and with all his strength, in accordance with all the Law of Moses (2 Kings 23:25).

Scripture: **2 Kings 23:21-25**
Song: **"The Greatest Thing in All My Life"**

Throughout the course of history, occasionally one individual stands out above the rest. The hall of fame list is long, of course, but here are some names that might immediately spring to mind: Moses, Alexander the Great, Augustine, Leonardo DaVinci, Abraham Lincoln, Albert Einstein. Each man's dedication to his life's purpose set them apart as the extraordinary, unique achievers they became. Although difficulties distracted them at times, they never lost sight of their dreams, pursuing them with everything they had.

Josiah won't be found in our secular history books, but God remembered him in His Book as one of the most extraordinary leaders who ever lived. This king hadn't led a great army or gathered tremendous wealth, but he did one thing that made him great: he kept sight of his determined purpose to be God's man.

Imagine having the king of the universe say, "There's never been one like you!" That's what separates the ordinary from the extraordinary in God's hall of fame.

Heavenly Father, *I want to follow You with all my heart. Give me the will and the strength to do it, one step at a time. In Jesus' name, amen.*

Wisdom Still Speaks

How much longer will you enjoy being stupid fools? Won't you ever stop sneering and laughing at knowledge? (Proverbs 1:22, *Contemporary English Version*).

Scripture: **Proverbs 1:20-33**
Song: **"O Boundless Wisdom, God Most High"**

It's becoming common in our modern society for true wisdom to be dismissed. Disguised, often thinly, as disdain for the traditional—or worse, "old-fashioned"—it's typically just the rejection of time-tested wisdom.

Today wisdom is often treated as a commodity that ebbs and flows according to the whims of culture and the popularity of trends, rather than standing on its own as something sacred. New studies, editorial opinions, scientific revelations, and strategically spun news reports—all can masquerade as authentic wisdom. So where shall we turn for genuine insight and good judgment?

In the book of Proverbs, wisdom is sometimes given a personality, as though it were actually a supernatural being alongside God at the time of creation. If we take the time to listen, wisdom's voice beckons, even today. In line at the grocery store, in traffic, at work . . . let us be alert to its matchless guidance.

Lord, *I have access to true wisdom through Your Spirit who dwells within me. Help me listen closely to His guidance today. In Jesus' name, amen.*

November 13–19. **Jeffrey Aran Leever** of Arvada, Colorado, is the author of *Even in Darkness* and *Daily Disciples.* He also contributes to Huskerpedia.com.

Why Won't They Listen?

Pay attention, my children! Follow my advice, and you will be happy (Proverbs 8:32, *Contemporary English Version*).

Scripture: **Proverbs 8:32-36**
Song: **"Listen to the Blessed Invitation"**

When it comes to listening, most of us have something in common. We've either made a parent wonder about the answer to the above title's question, or if we are a parent, we've asked it about our child.

As a youngster, far too often I disregarded the "pay attention" pleas issuing from my mother and teachers. Part of me knew the forthcoming information was important, that someone was trying to spare me from ignorance—or from getting into trouble. Still, the pleas usually failed to move me.

As an adult, I listen a little better, but sometimes God must still go to the extreme to grab my notice. This is strange, I suppose, because His Word clearly spells out the benefits of heeding Him: "You will be happy."

Seems like a pretty fair deal, doesn't it? Yet, as Benjamin Franklin once said: "He that won't be counseled can't be helped." Therefore, may we peel away the distractions of our eyes and the symphony of noise from our ears . . . and hear His caring voice. In the end, it is our lives that will benefit.

Dear Father, *I pray for clarity in hearing Your voice and the courage to follow all You say to me. I do thank You for granting me Your Spirit as counselor and guide through all my days on earth. In Jesus' name, amen.*

Today's Risky Business

Jeremiah, get ready! Go and tell the people what I command you to say. Don't be frightened by them (Jeremiah 1:17, *Contemporary English Version*).

Scripture: **Jeremiah 1:11-19**
Song: **"Be Bold"**

In our politically correct world, speaking out against wrongdoing takes more courage than ever. Christians today face a moral relativism that has turned traditional ethical formulations upside down. For example, only a few short decades ago, who could have imagined today's cultural outrage at the idea that sex be reserved only for marriage? Or the howls of protest at the suggestion that one religion might be more true than another?

When we feel that serious consequences loom, it's natural to want to avoid head-on collisions of worldview. Even Jeremiah must have had his fears about facing the evil of his day. But God told him to proceed with courage.

In this moment of quiet, I ask myself: How willing am I to point out wrongdoing, especially when I know I'll be called insensitive, offensive, or bigoted? We frequently long for guarantees that the risks will be worth it, that we'll succeed. But God has already given assurance in His Word: be faithful, and we will have our reward . . . here, or *there*.

Dear Lord, *make me a wise risk-taker for You, as Jeremiah was. Create in me a readiness and fearlessness to take on the challenges of a popular culture that abhors the idea of moral absolutes. In Christ's name I pray. Amen.*

Offer Refused!

But you refused to listen to my prophets . . . and you are the ones who were hurt by what you did (Jeremiah 25:7, *Contemporary English Version*).

Scripture: **Jeremiah 25:1-11**
Song: **"Not by Might"**

Hardened hearts keep more people out of Heaven than hardened arteries. The typical scenario goes like this: Something painful happens; a person feels wronged; bitterness follows but is pushed down and internalized. A heart becomes hardened to God. Admit it, we've all seen it. Or been there ourselves.

Later, God calls bitter people to repent and accept His love for them. Still, some people choose to reject His invitations, sometimes even blaming the voice that tried to help.

This is what happened to the prophet Jeremiah, a man who called the people of Judah (for 23 years!) to turn back to God from their idolatries. It certainly would have been much easier for Jeremiah just to blend in and ignore the evils around him. Yet he reminds us to speak out even amid a hostile and dangerous culture of unbelief.

We can debate whether or not Jeremiah actually made much difference; Judah's captivity ensued. But at least he presented the truth as God called him to do. Like him, we are simply to obey, leaving the results in God's hands.

Father, *I desire to communicate the gospel to lost people, regardless of the reception. Through the power of Christ's sacrifice, I pray. Amen.*

An Unfaithful Faith

All the leaders of the priests and the people became more and more unfaithful (2 Chronicles 36:14).

Scripture: **2 Chronicles 36:11-14**
Song: **"Believe Not Those Who Say"**

"Religion has not civilized man; man has civilized religion," said Robert Ingersoll, known as the King of American Orators in the mid-nineteenth century. He was also a committed agnostic.

Ingersoll was wrong about God's existence, but he was certainly right that human beings can attempt to "civilize" the true God, to make Him wishy-washy, tolerant of everything, and largely irrelevant. However, as our Scripture passage today demonstrates, worship of God requires exclusive faithfulness.

Sadly, many today wish to associate with Christ only superficially, as their so-called religious leaders continue moving away from reverence for God's teachings. It seems the more things change, the more they stay the same.

It's interesting to visit the Web site for secular humanism and find a great tribute to Robert Green Ingersoll (1833–1899). And, among the list of humanist affirmations there, we read: "We deplore efforts to explain the world in supernatural terms, and to look outside nature for salvation." What could be more unfaithful?

***God,** show me clearly what it means to live in faithfulness to You today. Guide me as I take each step. By the power of Jesus Christ, I pray. Amen.*

Our God: *Not* Safe!

They ignored what the LORD God was trying to tell them, until he finally became so angry that nothing could stop him (2 Chronicles 36:16, *Contemporary English Version*).

Scripture: **2 Chronicles 36:15-21**
Song: **"People Need the Lord"**

In an age of truth rejection, how far do we go to ensure that people get every chance to accept God's love? The task is so difficult because we now live under a different "covenant" than what was in place in 2 Chronicles: the philosophy of postmodernism. But in many ways the challenge is similar. God went to extraordinary lengths (through Jeremiah) to keep Jerusalem from destruction. Yet, even with God, there comes an end to restraint.

In one of C. S. Lewis's fiction books for children, *The Lion, the Witch and the Wardrobe,* Aslan the lion represents the person of Christ. Little Lucy contemplates what it will be like to meet him, asking: "Is he quite safe?"

The answer comes: "Safe? . . . Who said anything about safe? 'Course he isn't safe. But he's *good.* He's the King, I tell you." In another part of the book we read: "At the name of Aslan each one of the children felt something jump in his insides. Edmund felt a sensation of mysterious horror."

The love of God is gentle but never offered with a ticket to easy living. We do well to be in awe of Him.

Lord, *help me never take Your Word for granted. I love You—and I also reverence Your almighty name. Through Your beloved Son I pray. Amen.*

Righteous Indignation

Remember, O Lord, what the Edomites did on the day Jerusalem fell. "Tear it down," they cried, "tear it down to its foundations!" (Psalm 137:7).

Scripture: **Psalm 137**
Song: **"Let God Arise, and by His Might"**

You can't read the Bible for long without noticing the distinctly human tone of voice. The peaks and valleys of God's Word demonstrate a variety of emotions—very humanlike. And the psalmist's personal attachment to Jerusalem reflects God's long-suffering nature as well as a righteous indignation that longs for justice.

Have you encountered your own version of the Edomites in your life? If so, you know what it feels like to be misunderstood, mocked, and mistreated. Your soul then cries out for justice and the restoration of your dignity. Psalm 137 shows us that God has heard this type of angry, forlorn lament before.

While we're free to bring such pleas to His throne, God reminds us: "It is mine to avenge; I will repay" (Romans 12:19). Scripture never calls on us to carry out our own version of holy justice on God's behalf. Rather, we are invited to lay our burdens down before Him, trusting that His peace—a peace that transcends all understanding—will guard our hearts and our minds until everything is put right.

***Lord,** I weep for all that's wrong in the world, but I also thank You for promising to make all things new at the last day. Through Christ, amen.*

Driving Past Disaster

In you my soul takes refuge. I will take refuge in the shadow of your wings until the disaster has passed (Psalm 57:1).

Scripture: **Psalm 57**
Song: **"A Shelter in the Time of Storm"**

It was the last leg of our trip to Hot Springs, Arkansas, from Pennsylvania. On the outskirts of Little Falls, we saw the billboard advertising Carl's Motel. My boss's name was Carl, and since it was already late, I suggested, "Let's stay there and send Carl a postcard."

But we missed the exit, so we continued on to our destination though it was getting quite stormy before we settled into a motel in Hot Springs. The next morning we heard the news that a tornado had touched down in Little Falls. Curious to see the damages, we exited there on our return trip. Only the sign poles were left standing in the debris that had recently been . . . Carl's Motel.

According to the heading in my Bible, Psalm 57 was written to a tune called "Do Not Destroy." When the psalmist found refuge in the midst of disaster, his response was to sing and make music. As I drove through the storm-torn area, I prayed for those who experienced physical devastation. But I also offered a song of praise for the soul-keeping refuge of the Lord, my God.

Lord, *You spare me from so many dangers, most of which I never know. Praise to You, my shelter in the time of storm. Through Jesus I pray. Amen.*

November 20–26. **Penny Smith** of Harrisburg, Pennsylvania, has authored the books *Gateways to Growth* and *Keys to Christian Growth and Maturity.*

November 21

Personal Construction

It will be said: "Build up, build up, prepare the road! Remove the obstacles out of the way of my people" (Isaiah 57:14).

Scripture: **Isaiah 57:14-19**
Song: **"Builder of Ages"**

The construction for the new high school was a major undertaking, and radical changes to the whole area took place daily. Even the roadblocks and detours were constantly being changed—and our church sat right in the midst of it all.

The transformation that truly boggled my mind was the rerouting of a creek to create a new road. Each trip to church showed us the process, step by step. Workers removed trees and brush with earth-moving equipment, built up a solid foundation for the new road, and eventually tore out the old one. And the creek still flowed.

It's been said that we Christians are constantly under construction. Our creator-redeemer has given us the building materials. His Holy Spirit within us is our guide; the Bible is our blueprint. He may allow an interruption to slow us down, prevent us from financial crisis by blocking the approval of a loan, or clear the way for a new job. Divine diversions may be His pathway to our divine destiny. When crisis comes, praise Him for the comfort and restoration that is promised to follow.

Forgive me, Lord, *for complaining about unwanted changes in my life. Thank You that I am being built together with other believers to become a dwelling in which You live by Your Spirit. In Christ's name, amen.*

Productive Waiting

I wait for the Lord, my soul waits, and in his word I put my hope (Psalm 130:5).

Scripture: **Psalm 130**
Song: **"Be Still, My Soul"**

When it snows, my neighbor plows our shared driveway. But since he plows for many others, our driveway waits until the end of the day.

Once an unexpected snowstorm hit overnight, and I was to meet a friend at the airport in the morning. I prayed, "Lord, that plow needs to be here by 10:00 for me to get up the driveway." Of course, it wasn't my neighbor's custom to do such a thing. Besides, he knew nothing of my plight.

I was sorting laundry, wondering whom I could call upon to collect my friend on such a miserable day, when I heard a familiar engine roar. There was my neighbor, plowing the driveway. I checked the time. Exactly 10:00.

Waiting is one of the most strenuous spiritual challenges we face. The psalmist's posture seems to be one of inactivity. He says, "I wait . . . my soul waits." Then he reveals the key to his ability: he placed his hope in the Word of the Lord. But hoping, by faith, is hardly inactive; it is spiritual *exercise.* When we wait with an expectant posture, our belief is hard at work.

Teach me Your ways, Father, *so I can stretch the limbs of my spirit to embrace Your Word. As I learn to place all my hope in You, I thank You for every productive time of waiting in Your presence. In Jesus' name, amen.*

God Has a Plan

"I know the plans I have for you," declares the Lord, "plans to prosper you and not to harm you, plans to give you hope and a future" (Jeremiah 29:11).

Scripture: **Jeremiah 29:10-14**
Song: **"Hymn of Promise"**

She had filled our lives with chuckles and cheer, demonstrating what our senior years were meant to be. Whether speeding down the mountain on a snow slide, or dressing for a comedy act, she performed with superabundant joy and delight. Now she lay silenced by the brain tumor that had so quickly ravaged her life.

At first she would squeeze my hand to let me know she understood—and that she was still there. Now her hand lay limply in mine, death's dew formed on her brow.

It is one thing to trust the Lord for a bright future when you are in good health, but quite another when that health has failed. God doesn't tell us where our future lies or when our time on earth will end. Our confidence is in knowing that *all* of our times are in His capable hands.

While we remain here on earth, God's plans for us provide our hope for the future. If my friend could have responded in those last moments, I know that the squeeze of her hand would have indicated the strength of her confidence in our risen Lord.

Lord over all time, *because of Your great love for me, my future is bright. While I draw breath, keep my faith in You vibrant and confident, through all the changing seasons of my days. In Jesus' name I pray. Amen.*

The Upward Look

This is what Cyrus king of Persia says: "The Lord, the God of heaven . . . has appointed me to build a temple for him at Jerusalem in Judah. Anyone of his people among you—may the Lord his God be with him, and let him go up" (2 Chronicles 36:23).

Scripture: **2 Chronicles 36:22, 23**
Song: **"Let Zion's Watchmen All Awake"**

On my last visit to Israel, I learned that the house in which I stayed had been used as a blackout shelter during Operation Desert Storm in 1991. The occupants described how they had crowded into a dark inner hallway when the nightly curfew sounded. They would be there for hours, or even several days, hoping to avoid Saddam Hussein's Scud missile attacks.

When the all-clear signal sounded, they immediately left their hideout and climbed up the stairway to the roof above to assess any damage. What relief they felt upon going up, out of the darkened hiding place!

When I saw where they gathered, I could hardly believe they were able to exist there. But they passed the time by sharing stories, and also by turning their hearts' gaze upward—praying for one another and for the situation. Their prayers became proclamations of God's goodness, His protection, and His power. It made me think: is my heart propelled upward in the midst of trouble?

Heavenly Father, *I thank You for being the lifter of our heads, and for helping us to lift our eyes to You in the worst of times. In Jesus' name, amen.*

November 25

Packing to Move

Then rose up the chief of the fathers of Judah and Benjamin, and the priests, and the Levites, with all them whose spirit God had raised, to go up to build the house of the Lord which is in Jerusalem (Ezra 1:5, *King James Version*).

Scripture: **Ezra 1**
Song: **"Higher Ground"**

Some years ago I found myself in the embarrassing position of being homeless. Thankfully, it was for a short period of time, during which my hatchback car served as my official residence. I camped in style, moving about with a small mattress on the roof, my plasticware and a cook pot in the hatch with suitcases, my office in the back seat, and a dalmatian and dachshund in the passenger seat beside me. Don't ask me how we all fit.

The Lord had "raised my spirit," and I knew a time of preparation was at hand. I would sit on a park bench reading my Bible while the dogs exercised, and various passages would impress me: "Fear not." "Take no thought for your life." "Knock, and it shall be opened unto you." "Follow me." I had been stripped of most of my earthly possessions, dreams, and ambitions. Now it was time to rebuild.

Are you in transition? If so, there is no better time than this to prepare your heart and renew your mind for the next move. If you are following the Lord, He will provide.

***Father,** in times of uncertainty, lead me. Help me always to be willing to move if it serves Your kingdom purposes. Through Jesus I pray. Amen.*

Do Not Enter!

We are the servants of the God of heaven and earth, and we are rebuilding the temple that was built many years ago, one that a great king of Israel built and finished (Ezra 5:11).

Scripture: **Ezra 5:6-14**
Song: **"I Will Go in the Strength of the Lord"**

Have you ever innocently entered a room, only to discover that you were in an Authorized Personnel Only area? With my poor sense of direction, this has taken many forms for me. For instance, I once not only entered a gent's rest room but actually started into a stall before I realized it. I've entered the exit ramp in parking garages, and then tried to exit the entrance ramp. I've tried to make my key work in someone else's locker, rushed into a private courtroom, and absentmindedly invaded the restricted area of an airport. Where will I end up next?

In a few of the above scenarios, I immediately heard the question posed to Ezra's temple builders: "Who has authorized you to be here?" I'd cringe, stutter, and back out with a red face.

On the other hand, when we're moving in the authority that has been given us, we enter the privileged places with confidence. As Christians, we are to walk in the authority that is ours through the sacrifice of Christ. We are indeed servants of the God of Heaven and earth, just as were the workers of Ezra's day.

Heavenly Father, *may the authority of the resurrection power of Christ empower me to do Your will today. In Jesus' name, amen.*

November 27

Precious Gift

They had no children, because Elizabeth was barren; and they were both well along in years (Luke 1:7).

Scripture: **Luke 1:5-20**
Song: **"Happy the Home When God Is There"**

Married for three years, both were in their late 30s. Although they were anxious to start a family, pregnancy eluded them. As a last resort, they tried in vitro fertilization. But when that failed, the doctor asked, "Would you consider adoption?" Instead, they traveled to another hospital in another state. And nine months later they became the parents of a beautiful, eight-pound baby girl.

The in vitro procedure was expensive, exhausting, and risky. Yet the happy couple says, "It was worth every cost, every obstacle. We are so thankful for God's goodness."

Zechariah and Elizabeth, dutiful servants of the Lord, had longed for, and prayed for, a child. But time had passed, and perhaps they had resigned themselves to being childless. Can you imagine Zechariah's astonishment and disbelief when the angel of the Lord appeared to announce their desire would be granted? And this child would be a key player in God's redemptive plan, preparing the people for Christ's coming. This couple too offered thanks for the goodness of God.

Gracious God, *praise to You for the children among us. May every parent be reminded this day: how precious are these gifts! Through Christ, amen.*

November 27–30. **Cos Barnes,** of Southern Pines, North Carolina, is a mother of three and grandmother of seven. She enjoys playing handbells for her church.

The Benefits of Silence

When he came out, he could not speak to them. They realized he had seen a vision in the temple, for he kept making signs to them but remained unable to speak (Luke 1:22).

Scripture: **Luke 1:21-25**
Song: **"Silently the Shades of Evening"**

My friend Sandra's parents were both deaf, her father from birth, her mother from the age of 6. She tells me they had no telephone until she was 8 years old. At that time, Sandra became her parents' communicator, the one who phoned for doctor's appointments, car inspections, or prescription deliveries. The three of them used sign language to communicate, so Sandra grew up in a silent household—which had its limitations and benefits.

Zechariah learned about silence the hard way. He was made unable to speak from the time the angel Gabriel appeared until the day the promised son entered the world. After the angelic encounter, Zechariah could only sign and gesture to the worshipers outside the temple.

I have a feeling that after he returned home and somehow conveyed his miraculous encounter to Elizabeth, Zechariah spent the next nine months in prayerful thanksgiving. He knew the limitations of silence, but surely over the years of observing his son John's ministry, he must have reveled in its awesome benefits.

Dear God, *I pray today for people who are deaf or hard of hearing. I know sometimes they feel alone and isolated. Please help them know how special they are to You. In Christ's holy name I pray. Amen.*

Fatherly Preparation

You, my child, will be called a prophet of the Most High; for you will go on before the Lord to prepare the way for him (Luke 1:76).

Scripture: **Luke 1:67-80**
Song: **"Prepare the Way, O Zion!"**

After the birth of their child, Zechariah praised God not only for sending a son but for providing salvation for the world. Directing his words to his son, Zechariah told John he would give knowledge and salvation to the people and prepare the way of the Lord. John the Baptist would be the forerunner of Jesus and would acquaint the people with God, for they really did not know what He was like.

I've noticed how fathers take pride in their sons. They are just as proud of their daughters, of course. But there seems to be a special father-son relationship in mentoring a boy into manhood—something a mom can't accomplish.

I witnessed it when my husband and son would discuss football strategy, school relationships, business tactics, and marital challenges. I remember their early games of catch and my husband demonstrating the butterfly stroke, removing the training wheels when it was time, and fixing the flats on both bike and car. Dad was always there with mature guidance when trouble loomed. He served as best man at his boy's wedding and soon babysat the grandchildren. The cycle starts once again.

***Thank You** for parents who faithfully guide sons and daughters in righteousness. Give them wisdom and strength this day. Through Christ, amen.*

Shout the Good News

People went out to him from Jerusalem and all Judea and the whole region of the Jordan (Matthew 3:5).

Scripture: **Matthew 3:1-6**
Song: **"Gospel Echoes"**

John came proclaiming the Messiah. Living in the wilderness, John was dressed in coarse attire and spoke in no-nonsense words to the multitudes who came to hear him. Appealing to their intellects, as well as their hearts, he stressed repentance because the kingdom of Heaven was at hand. The penitents, after confessing their sins, received baptism from John, the water signifying God's gracious gift: cleansing from sin.

John was privileged to prepare the people for Christ's appearance, and he had great influence with them. We too have influence with people, even when we are unaware of its full extent. But we can go beyond this passive influence to have an active, positive witness.

By our words, and also by our actions, we can joyfully proclaim the goodness of God in our lives, clearly identifying ourselves as servants of King Jesus. We may feel as if we're in the wilderness when we do so. And the crowds may not go out to us. But look for that person—here . . . there—who seems to have an open heart. He or she is ready for your life-giving testimony. Let it bubble forth loud and clear.

God, *keep me alert to people around me today. May I catch the eye of one whose heart You have prepared for good news. In Jesus' name, amen.*

My Prayer Notes